COMING TO CHRIST

A STUDY OF THE
DETAILED CONVERSIONS
IN ACTS

COMING TO CHRIST

A STUDY OF THE DETAILED CONVERSIONS IN ACTS

AARON ERHARDT

EP

ERHARDT PUBLICATIONS

Louisville, Kentucky
2009

DEDICATION

To our children, Skylar and Luke.
They have brought great joy to our lives.
May they mature into faithful servants of the Lord Jesus,
and never waver in their service to Him.

Also Dedicated To:

Ron Daly
Don Wright
J. R. Bronger

CONTENTS

FOREWORD

Apart from the gospels, which tell of our Savior and His sacrifice, no book of the Bible is of greater instructional importance than that of the book of Acts, for it is Acts that tells us how to respond to the message of the gospels. And, a response is vital; the life and death of Jesus Christ has no meaning if there is not a response from sinful men.

But, how do we respond — that is the question, isn't it? Men have wrestled with that question for centuries on end. What does God expect man to do in order to avail himself of the redemptive work of Christ? Answers have been as varied as men are. Some say we must work our way to heaven. Others say that we are predestined regardless of choices we may make. Still others say that we are saved by grace alone. Some say that we must be either immersed or sprinkled with water. All these answers come from well-meaning and often learned people. What is a sinner to do?

Enter the Acts of the Apostles. In this book, we find people like ourselves exposed to the message of the gospel — that they are sinners and lost, but Christ died to take away their sins if they will only "Come to Me" (Matthew 11:28). Luke, the historian who wrote this book, tells us, in strikingly vivid and precise details, exactly how these sinners became saints.

Aaron Erhardt has been a preacher of the gospel and friend for many years. He has a passion for clear and simple Bible preaching. The use of the word "simple" is in no way derogatory; far from it, for simplicity in preaching is often a hard destination for a preacher or teacher to find. Having come out of denominationalism, Aaron understands the pitfalls of complicated arguments proposed by men over the centuries — arguments designed to overlook the intended message of scripture in favor of the coveted doctrines of men. Aaron takes a straightforward, and in many ways radical, approach: Let's just examine the text and see how people became Christians at the genesis of the church. Each detailed account of conversion is examined, first letting the text speak for itself, then Aaron supplies any relevant additional information — historical backgrounds, geographical information, etc. — that may be helpful to understanding the message given or actions taking place. When the Bible stands alone, without the filters of men's doctrines, I believe the truth will be clear. This book is a wonderful tool in one's quest for the truth.

So, if you have picked up this book with the intention of seeking truth to obey yourself or teach to others, and you are willing to put aside any preconceived ideas and simply look at the stories of salvation found in this narrative, then prepare to be challenged with the simplicity and consistency of Luke's account. I am thankful my brother has worked to prepare this helpful volume.

Mark McCrary

INTRODUCTION

The book of Acts is the second part of a two-volume work. It picks up where the Gospel of Luke ends. Together, these two volumes cover a period of more than sixty years and comprise more than one-fourth of the New Testament. Acts does not record all of the acts that the apostles performed, or even most of them. Instead the Holy Spirit selected a few acts to be recorded for us. Peter's work primarily dominates the first half of the book (Acts 1-12) while Paul's work dominates the latter half (Acts 13-28). Three of Paul's missionary journeys are recorded in Acts (Acts 13:1-14:28; 15:40-18:22; 18:23-21:17), and his journey to Rome.

The book of Acts gives us a great deal of information about the history of the church, including its establishment and expansion in the first century. It records the initial fulfillment of the Great Commission (Matthew 28:19-20), beginning in Jerusalem and spreading throughout the Roman Empire. Acts also sheds enormous light upon the epistles, which allows us to more fully understand them.

The book of Acts rehearses how the message was successfully proclaimed by the apostles and others (2:41; 4:4; 5:14; 6:1, 7; 8:6; 9:31, 42; 11:21, 24; 12:24; 13:43; 14:1, 21; 16:5; 17:4; 18:8; 19:20), and how baptized believers joined together to form local churches. Those churches soon appointed elders to guide and protect the flock (Acts 11:30; 14:23; 15:2, 4, 6, 22-23; 16:4; 20:17; 21:18). The one-man rule that is so prevalent in denominations today was unknown in the book of Acts. Local churches were organized with a plurality of elders.

Acts details how early churches came together on the first day of the week to break bread (Acts 20:7). This act of worship was instituted by the Lord to commemorate his death until he comes again (1 Corinthians 11:23-26). There was no such thing as a monthly or quarterly observance of the Lord's Supper in the first century, they broke bread weekly.

Acts demonstrates that the gospel message is for all men, both Jew and Gentile (Acts 1:8). All those who hear and obey the truth are accepted by God, regardless of race, rank, or nationality (Acts 10:34-35). There is no partiality or prejudice. *The ground is completely level at the foot of the cross!*

As one might expect, the death and resurrection of Christ are frequently mentioned by various speakers throughout the book of Acts (2:23-24; 3:15; 4:10; 5:30; 7:52; 8:32-35; 10:39-40; 13:28-30). The return of Christ and final judgment are also mentioned (1:11; 3:20-21; 10:42; 17:31; 23:6; 24:15, 25; 26:7-8).

Jesus is presented in Acts as vindicated and exalted. He is the risen Savior who sits at the right hand of God. Jesus is referred to in many ways, including Lord, Christ, Son of God, Holy and Righteous One, Son of Man, Author of life, Leader and Savior, and judge of the living and the dead.

The book of Acts is a book of sermons. About 300 verses are devoted to sermon material. There are ten *major* sermons recorded (2:14-40; 3:12-26; 7:1-60; 10:28-48; 13:16-41; 17:22-31; 20:18-35; 22:1-21; 24:10-21; 26:1-29). Six of those sermons were preached by Paul, three by Peter, and one by Stephen.

Acts is also a book of conversions, which is the main focus of the book before you. We see exactly how lost souls were saved in the first century. The question of questions "What must I do to be saved?" is answered in clear terms. Upon hearing the message proclaimed, believers responded to it in humble obedience by repenting of their sins, confessing their faith in Christ, and being baptized for the forgiveness of sins.

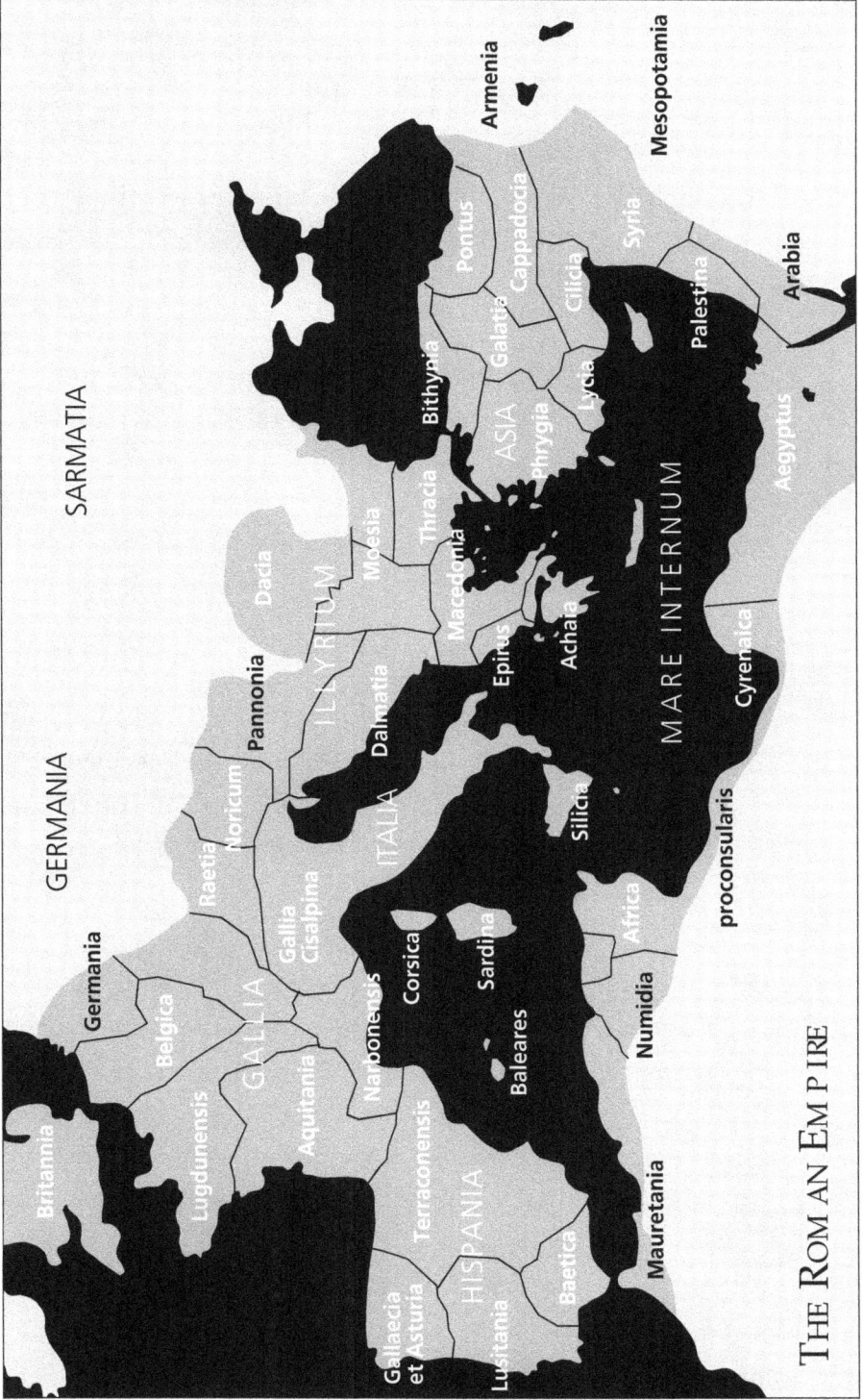

SARMATIA

GERMANIA

Armenia

Mesopotamia

Britannia

Germania

Belgica

GALLIA

Lugdunensis

Aquitania

Narbonensis

Terraconensis

HISPANIA

Gallaedia et Asturia

Lusitania

Baetica

Raetia

Noricum

Gallia Cisalpina

ITALIA

ILLYRIUM

Pannonia

Dacia

Moesia

Dalmatia

Thracia

Bithynia

Macedonia

Epirus

Achaia

Pontus

Cappadocia

Galatia

ASIA

Phrygia

Cilicia

Lycia

Syria

Palestina

Arabia

Aegyptus

MARE INTERNUM

Cyrenaica

Corsica

Sardinia

Baleares

Silicia

Africa proconsularis

Numidia

Mauretania

THE ROMAN EMPIRE

WRITER

Although the writer does not identify himself, it is easy through internal and external evidence to determine that Luke wrote the book of Acts.

(1) The writer had previously written to Theophilus and this volume was a follow-up to it. Only Luke is known to have written to Theophilus (Luke 1:3).

(2) There are 58 words used in Luke and Acts that are not used in any other place in the New Testament. The similarities in language and style are also striking.

(3) The writer was a frequent companion of Paul. There are many passages that say "we" and "us" in the book, indicating that the writer was present with Paul on certain journeys (Acts 16:10-17; 20:5-21:18; 27:1-28:16). That would certainly be true of Luke.

(4) Irenaeus, Clement of Alexandria, Tertullian, Origen, Eusebius, and other early writers name Luke as the writer.

(5) The earliest known list of the New Testament writings, the Muratorian Fragment, names Luke as the writer.

All of these points confirm that Luke wrote the book of Acts. Most believe he wrote it in Rome during Paul's first Roman imprisonment in A. D. 62.

LUKE

Luke is only mentioned by name three times in the New Testament (Colossians 4:14; 2 Timothy 4:11; Philemon 24). From those texts, we learn that he was a Gentile physician who frequently journeyed with Paul and assisted him during his imprisonments. According to tradition, Luke was born in Antioch of Syria. That may explain why he showed so much interest in Antioch in the book of Acts. He may have lived in Philippi as an adult since he stayed there when Paul left during his second missionary journey and was still there when Paul returned during his third missionary journey. Some suggest that Luke was the brother of Titus, although that cannot be proven.

THEOPHILUS

Both Luke and Acts are addressed to a man named Theophilus. Although we are not given much information about him, the words "most excellent" (Luke 1:3) were commonly used in addressing Roman officials (Acts 23:26; 24:2; 26:25). Therefore, it is possible that Theophilus was an official of the Roman Empire. Some suggest that the omission of the words "most excellent" before his name in Acts may indicate that Theophilus became a Christian as a result of reading the Gospel of Luke, and either resigned or was removed from his position by the time Acts was written. While that may be true, there is not enough evidence to support that suggestion with any real certainty.

Since the name Theophilus means "lover of God," some have supposed that Luke was not writing to any particular individual, but to anyone who loves God. However, the title "most excellent" seems to indicate that he was referring to an actual person. It is also worth noting that Theophilus was a common name.

HOLY SPIRIT

The book of Acts could accurately be called the "Acts of the Holy Spirit" because of how active he is in the book. He empowered the apostles on Pentecost (2:4), directed preachers (8:29), comforted churches (9:31), selected missionaries (13:2), presided over the Jerusalem meeting (15:28), and much more.

The Holy Spirit is the third person of the Godhead (Matthew 3:16-17; 28:19-20; Acts 5:3-4). He hears (John 16:13), speaks (1 Timothy 4:1), teaches (John 14:26), communes (2 Corinthians 13:14), comforts (Acts 9:31), leads (Romans 8:14), loves (Romans 15:30), testifies (John 15:26), and bears witness (Romans 8:16). He can be lied to (Acts 5:3), grieved (Ephesians 4:30), blasphemed (Matthew 12:31), resisted (Acts 7:51), quenched (1 Thessalonians 5:19), and outraged (Hebrews 10:29). He has a will (1 Corinthians 12:11) and knowledge (1 Corinthians 2:11).

The book of Acts is an invaluable part of God's Word. It contains so much important information that one can hardly imagine the New Testament without it. With that said, it is with all humility that I present the book before you on the detailed conversions in Acts.

CHAPTER 1

THE JEWS ON PENTECOST

Just before his ascension into heaven, Jesus instructed the apostles to wait in Jerusalem for the coming of the Holy Spirit. This coming would supernaturally empower them to carry out their mission of preaching the gospel message to the world.

But you will receive power when the Holy Spirit has come upon you, and you will be my witnesses in Jerusalem and in all Judea and Samaria, and to the end of the earth (Acts 1:8)

The Holy Spirit came upon the apostles ten days later, on the feast day of Pentecost. Pentecost, called the "Feast of Weeks" and "Feast of Harvest" in the Old Testament, was one of three annual feasts that Jews were required to attend in Jerusalem. The others were Passover and Tabernacles. Pentecost, which means fiftieth, was celebrated fifty days after Passover. It was a time of rejoicing and thanksgiving for the bountiful crops that they were beginning to harvest. Pentecost always fell on the first day of the week. This was the first Pentecost after the crucifixion of Jesus.

When the day of Pentecost arrived, they were all together in one place. And suddenly there came from heaven a sound like a mighty rushing wind, and it filled the entire house where they were sitting. And divided tongues as of fire appeared to them and rested on each one of them. And they were all filled with the Holy

Spirit and began to speak in other tongues as the Spirit gave them utterance (Acts 2:1-4)

Jerusalem was overflowing with people on Pentecost. It has been estimated that the population in the city swelled to nearly a million during the feast. In fact, there were so many Jews in Jerusalem during this time that Roman governors, fearing a spontaneous revolt, brought in extra troops for security. It is no wonder that God chose Pentecost to begin the work of preaching the gospel to the world (Mark 16:15). The place was packed! The symbolism in beginning the harvest of souls on the feast day celebrating the harvest is also unmistakable.

Contrary to what many teach, only the apostles were filled with the Holy Spirit on Pentecost. Acts 1 ends with Matthias being numbered "with the eleven apostles" (v. 26). Then Acts 2 begins with the pronouns "they" and "them," which point back to the antecedent "apostles." There are other clear indications as well. (1) The promise of Holy Spirit baptism was made to the apostles (Acts 1:5). (2) Those baptized in the Spirit were all Galileans (Acts 2:7). (3) Only Peter and the eleven stood up to speak (Acts 2:14). (4) The Jews directed their question to the apostles (Acts 2:37). Only the apostles were filled with the Holy Spirit that day.

After being filled with the Holy Spirit, the apostles miraculously began speaking in different tongues (or languages) they had never studied before.

Now there were dwelling in Jerusalem Jews, devout men from every nation under heaven. And at this sound the multitude

came together, and they were bewildered, because each one was hearing them speak in his own language. And they were amazed and astonished, saying, "Are not all these who are speaking Galileans? And how is it that we hear, each of us in his own native language? Parthians and Medes and Elamites and residents of Mesopotamia, Judea and Cappadocia, Pontus and Asia, Phrygia and Pamphylia, Egypt and the parts of Libya belonging to Cyrene, and visitors from Rome, both Jews and proselytes, Cretans and Arabians—we hear them telling in our own tongues the mighty works of God" (Acts 2:5-10)

Tongue speaking was a miraculous gift in the early church that allowed the speaker to communicate in languages he had never studied before. That tongues were actual languages is proven by the context in Acts 2: "began to speak in other tongues...each one was hearing them speak in his own language...how is it that we hear, each of us in his own native language" (vv. 4, 6, 8). Tongues were not some ecstatic utterance or gibberish, which is so prevalent within the holiness movement today. They were known languages!

The Gift of Tongues
- Miraculous gift that allowed speaker to communicate in language never studied before (Acts 2:4-8)
- In assembly, tongue speakers were to speak one at a time, and only two or three could speak in any given service (1 Corinthians 14:27)
- All miraculous gifts, including tongues, ceased when New Testament was completed (1 Corinthians 13:8-10)
- Chrysostom, Augustine, and other early writers considered tongues obsolete

It is important to note that those given the gift of tongues in the early church did not have to be taught how to use the gift by others. There were no tongue-rolling exercises, lesson books, or seminars. They simply spoke "as the Spirit gave them utterance."

Having gained the attention of the multitude, Peter and the eleven stood up to proclaim the message of Jesus Christ to the Jews.

Peter, standing with the eleven, lifted up his voice and addressed them (Acts 2:14)

Peter, originally named Simon, was one of the original twelve apostles, and often acted as the leader of the group. In fact, his name appears first in every list of the Twelve (Matthew 10:2-4; Mark 3:16-19; Luke 6:14-16; Acts 1:13). His brother Andrew was also an apostle. Peter was a fisherman by trade. He was married and had children. He wrote two epistles in the New Testament and died a martyr's death, which the Lord foretold (John 21:18-19). Peter's name is mentioned more in the gospels than any other name except Jesus.

Peter also served as an elder in a local church (1 Peter 5:1). Elders were appointed to guide and protect the flock. Though an apostle, Peter was not above serving in a local capacity!

Peter was impetuous and inquisitive. He asked more questions in the gospels than all of the other apostles combined. He was also part of the Lord's inner circle, along with James and John (Matthew 17:1; Mark 5:37; 13:3; 14:33).

Among the many things that attest to the fact that Jesus was raised from the dead is the sudden transformation of the apostles from weak and cowardly to strong and courageous. This was especially true of Peter. Just weeks earlier he had denied even knowing the Lord, now he stood boldly before a large audience of Jews and declared Jesus to be the Christ. If Jesus were not really resurrected, how do we explain Peter's sudden transformation? We don't. The only logical explanation is that Peter saw the resurrected Lord!

Finally living up to his name, Peter spoke to the Jews with rock-solid conviction.

Men of Israel, hear these words: Jesus of Nazareth, a man attested to you by God with mighty works and wonders and signs that God did through him in your midst, as you yourselves know—this Jesus, delivered up according to the definite plan and foreknowledge of God, you have crucified and killed by the hands of lawless men. God raised him up, loosing the pangs of death, because it was not possible for him to be held by it. For David says concerning him, "I saw the Lord always before me, for he is at my right hand that I may not be shaken; therefore my heart was glad, and my tongue rejoiced; my flesh also will dwell in hope. For you will not abandon my soul to Hades, or let your Holy One see corruption. You have made known to me the paths of life; you will make me full of gladness with your presence." Brothers, I may say to you with confidence about the patriarch David that he both died and was buried, and his tomb is with us to this day. Being therefore a prophet, and knowing that God had sworn with an oath to him that he would set one of his descendants on his throne, he foresaw and spoke about the resurrection of the Christ, that he was not

abandoned to Hades, nor did his flesh see corruption. This Jesus God raised up, and of that we are all witnesses. Being therefore exalted at the right hand of God, and having received from the Father the promise of the Holy Spirit, he has poured out this that you yourselves are seeing and hearing. For David did not ascend into the heavens, but he himself says, "The Lord said to my Lord, Sit at my right hand, until I make your enemies your footstool." Let all the house of Israel therefore know for certain that God has made him both Lord and Christ, this Jesus whom you crucified (Acts 2:22-36)

Many of those present on Pentecost had witnessed the crucifixion of Jesus. They were part of the angry mob that cried out for his death. That makes it all the more impressive to hear Peter proclaim the message of Jesus Christ to the Jews and accuse them of having blood on their hands. The fear was gone. The message was clear. The Jews murdered the Messiah, and Peter let them know it! He rehearsed how Jesus performed miracles in their midst, was delivered up, crucified, and resurrected as predicted in the Old Testament. The death and resurrection of Christ was the central theme of Peter's preaching throughout the book of Acts (Acts 3:15; 4:10; 5:30; 10:39-40).

The Jews, who had probably heard whispers that Jesus was raised from the dead, were convicted by the message. They believed what Peter said and immediately sought forgiveness.

Now when they heard this they were cut to the heart, and said to Peter and the rest of the apostles, "Brothers, what shall we do?" (Acts 2:37)

The Jews were cut to the heart and asked how to be forgiven. This indicates belief on their part. The word "cut" *(katenygesan)* means to pierce or to strike. The gospel penetrated their hearts like a sharp arrow. This is the only time that the word appears in the New Testament.

The question of the crowd on Pentecost is reminiscent of the questions John the baptizer received from the crowds during his ministry (Luke 3:10, 12, 14). In both instances, the people asked, "What shall we do?" Peter wasted no time answering their question!

And Peter said to them, "Repent and be baptized every one of you in the name of Jesus Christ for the forgiveness of your sins, and you will receive the gift of the Holy Spirit. For the promise is for you and for your children and for all who are afar off, everyone whom the Lord our God calls to himself" (Acts 2:38-39)

The Greek preposition "for" *(eis)* means in order to obtain. It looks ahead to a result. The Jews were told to repent and be baptized in order to obtain the forgiveness of sins. The same is still true today. Upon believing, one must repent, which is a change of mind that results in a change of life, and be baptized.

The "gift of the Holy Spirit" in this text must be distinguished from the miraculous gifts imparted by the laying on of the apostles' hands. The reason for this is because those gifts were not given to every baptized believer. However, in this text the gift is for every baptized believer. What then is the gift of the Spirit? I believe it is simply the gift of salvation promised by the Spirit (v. 21).

Just as the same sun melts butter and hardens concrete, so it is with the gospel message upon the hearts of men. It will either melt the heart or harden it. In this case, many of the Jews had their hearts melted and responded favorably to the conditions set forth by Peter.

So those who received his word were baptized, and there were added that day about three thousand souls (Acts 2:41)

Nothing can take away sin except the precious blood of Jesus Christ. We contact that blood when we are baptized. In other words, the blood is *what* takes away our sins; baptism is *when* it takes away our sins. Consider the chart below.

Blood	Baptism
Remits (Matthew 26:28)	Remits (Acts 2:38)
Washes (Revelation 1:5)	Washes (Acts 22:16)
Cleanses (1 John 1:7)	Cleanses (Ephesians 5:26)
Saves (Romans 5:9)	Saves (1 Peter 3:21) KJV

About 3,000 Jews on Pentecost had their sins forgiven. They were saved by the blood of Christ through their obedience to the gospel message. There was nothing said about a "sinner's prayer" or "justification by faith only." Saving faith is an obedient faith.

The fact that 3,000 people were baptized in *one* day indicates that baptism was extremely important in the first century. It was not to be delayed or postponed. The reason denominations wait days or weeks to baptize someone is because they believe baptism is not necessary. The reason the apostles baptized 3,000 in one day is because they believed baptism was necessary!

It is important for us to note just how the Holy Spirit worked in the conversion of the Jews on Pentecost. He worked through the Word: "Began to speak" (v. 4), "hearing them speak" (v. 6), "give ear to my words" (v. 14), "hear these words" (v. 22), "when they heard this" (v. 37), "Peter said" (v. 38), "with many other words" (v. 40), "received his word" (v. 41). The Jews were converted by the Spirit through the Word. It is his means or medium of operation (Ephesians 6:17).

In Caesarea Philippi, Jesus promised Peter that he would be given "the keys of the kingdom" (Matthew 16:19). Keys are used to open doors. Now we see Peter using those keys to open the doors of the kingdom to the Jews. Acts 2 marks the beginning of the New Testament era and the much anticipated kingdom of Christ (Daniel 2:44; Mark 1:15; 9:1). It is the birthday of the Lord's church!

Some argue that the church was established during the earthly ministry of Christ. If that were so, it had no blood (John 19:34), no head (Ephesians 1:22), no completed gospel (1 Corinthians 15:1-4), no redemption (Hebrews 9:15), and no new covenant (Hebrews 9:16-17). Furthermore, it would have existed under the limited commission, and its members could not have gloried in the cross. Who can believe such a thing? Not until Acts 2, after the death and resurrection of Christ, was the church established.

Review

Day of Pentecost in Jerusalem

Apostles filled with Holy Spirit

Message proclaimed by apostles

About 3,000 repented and were baptized

The Lord's church was established

CHAPTER 2

THE SAMARITANS

The church grew rapidly in Jerusalem. Thousands were rendering their obedience to the gospel message, including "a great many of the priests" (Acts 6:7). That growth did not go unnoticed among the Jewish leaders who felt threatened by it. They ordered the apostles to stop speaking in the name of Jesus. When that did not work, they steadily intensified their efforts. The persecution escalated from verbal threats to physical beatings and then murder.

Then they cast him [Stephen] out of the city and stoned him. And the witnesses laid down their garments at the feet of a young man named Saul (Acts 7:58)

Stephen was one of the seven chosen to tend to the physical needs of the widows in the Jerusalem church (Acts 6). His name seems to suggest that he was a Hellenist, meaning he was among the Jews that had accepted at least some Greek customs. He was a man "of good repute, full of the Spirit and of wisdom" (Acts 6:3). He boldly proclaimed the gospel message to the Jews. Unlike Pentecost, however, the message was rejected and the preacher was killed.

With the persecution against the church getting more and more intense, many of the disciples in Jerusalem fled elsewhere. They did not leave empty-handed, however. They took the gospel message with them!

And there arose on that day a great persecution against the church in Jerusalem, and they were all scattered throughout the regions of Judea and Samaria, except the apostles...Now those who were scattered went about preaching the word (Acts 8:1, 4)

God has a way of working things out for good. We see that with Joseph being sold into slavery by his brothers (Genesis 50:20) and with Paul being imprisoned in Rome (Philippians 1:12-14). In both instances, an apparent bad situation ended up accomplishing good. The same is true here. The disciples scattering from Jerusalem seemed to be a victory for the Devil, but it ended up helping to promote Christ in other places. The disciples scattered with the gospel message, thus enabling an even larger audience to hear about Jesus!

Interestingly, this is one of only three times that the word "persecution" appears in the book of Acts (11:19; 13:50). Luke underscores the degree of persecution by inserting the word "great." This persecution was very severe!

Since the Jerusalem church continued to exist after this scattering (Acts 9:26; 11:2, 22; 12:1, 5; 15:4; 21:17), we should probably understand "all" as simply meaning that many of the disciples scattered from Jerusalem.

Among those who scattered was Philip. Like Stephen, he had been one of the seven men chosen to tend to the physical needs of widows in the Jerusalem church. He was full of the Holy Spirit and wisdom (Acts 6:3). We know this was not Philip the apostle because the apostles remained in Jerusalem (Acts 8:1), and because Peter and John had to come lay hands on the Samaritans to impart the miraculous gifts. If this were Philip the apostle, the other apostles would not have needed to come. He could have done it himself. This was "Philip the evangelist" (Acts 21:8). Philip took the message to an unnamed city in Samaria.

Philip went down to the city of Samaria and proclaimed to them the Christ (Acts 8:5)

Jerusalem was situated on a high plateau. Therefore, those leaving Jerusalem were always said to go down (v. 15), while those entering the city were always said to go up (Acts 25:9). Samaria was actually located to the north of Jerusalem.

Most Jews despised the Samaritans. They considered them half-breeds cursed by God because of their mixed ancestry, and even used the term "Samaritan" as an insult (John 8:48). In fact, when Jesus was looking for the most reviled figure his Jewish audience could imagine in order to make a point about neighborly love, he chose a Samaritan (Luke 10:33). This makes the entrance of Philip into Samaria all the more impressive. He was impartial with the gospel message!

The gospel going to the Samaritans would only fan the flames of anger among the Jewish leaders in Jerusalem. It would be like pouring alcohol on an open wound. If it were not bad enough that Jews were receiving the message, now the hated Samaritans were receiving it also.

The Samaritans were captivated by the words and wonders of Philip. He no doubt received the power to do such wonders, which included the ability to cast out unclean spirits and to heal the crippled, when the apostles laid hands on him in Acts 6:6. Joy was in the air!

And the crowds with one accord paid attention to what was being said by Philip when they heard him and saw the signs he did. For unclean spirits came out of many who were possessed, crying with a loud voice, and many who were paralyzed or lame were healed. So there was much joy in that city (Acts 8:6-8)

Like Stephen (Acts 6:8), Philip had the power to perform miraculous gifts, which Luke calls "signs" (Acts 2:19, 22, 43; 4:16, 22, 30; 5:12; 6:8; 7:36; 8:6, 13; 14:3; 15:12). The miraculous gifts were imparted by the laying on of the apostles' hands (Acts 8:17-18; 19:6; Romans 1:11), and were designed to confirm the message (Mark 16:20; John 20:30-31; Hebrews 2:3-4) until the New Testament was completed (1 Corinthians 13:8-10). In other words, when the age of revelation came to a close, the miraculous gifts ceased also. They were never intended to be a permanent practice in the church.

Like the Jews on Pentecost, many of the Samaritans were obedient to the gospel message. They believed and were baptized.

But when they believed Philip as he preached good news about the kingdom of God and the name of Jesus Christ, they were baptized, both men and women (Acts 8:12)

Amazing! The Samaritans, whom the Jews despised, were now citizens in the kingdom of God. They were recipients of the spiritual blessings in Christ.

It is important to note that men and women were baptized, not infants and toddlers. New Testament baptism is for those who are capable of hearing and heeding the message. Consider the chart below.

New Testament Baptism	Infant Baptism
Taught (Matthew 28:19)	Untaught
Believers (Mark 16:16)	Unbelievers
Repentant (Acts 2:38)	Unrepentant
Men and Women (Acts 8:12)	Infants
Confessors (Acts 8:37)	Non-Confessors
Sinners (Acts 22:16)	Sinless KJV

From the above chart we see that an infant is not a proper candidate for baptism. He cannot be taught, believe, repent, or confess. Nor is he in sin (Ezekiel 18:20).

Perhaps we should take a moment to address the "household" conversions in Acts since they are often used to defend infant baptism.

Cornelius. His household feared God (Acts 10:2), heard the message (Acts 10:33), believed the message (Acts 11:17), and had their hearts purified by faith (Acts 15:9). Infants cannot do those things.

Lydia. Although we are not told much about her household, one would have to assume that she was married, had children, had *infant* children, and that her infant children were with her at the time of her conversion. You cannot build a doctrine of mere assumptions.

Philippian Jailor. His household heard the message (Acts 16:32), believed the message (Acts 16:34), and rejoiced that they were saved (Acts 16:34). Infants cannot do those things.

Crispus. His household believed the message (Acts 18:8). Infants cannot do that.

Stephanas. His household devoted themselves to the service of the saints (1 Corinthians 16:15). Infants cannot do that.

There is no evidence from the "household" conversions to support the practice of infant baptism. There is neither precept nor example of infant baptism in the New Testament.

There was a man in Samaria named Simon. He practiced magic, which was nothing less than witchcraft. Such magicians were common in those days (Acts 13:6). He deceived many of the people into believing that he was invested with supernatural power from God.

But there was a man named Simon, who had previously practiced magic in the city and amazed the people of Samaria, saying that he himself was somebody great. They all paid attention to him, from the least to the greatest, saying, "This man is the power of God that is called Great." And they paid attention to him because for a long time he had amazed them with his magic (Acts 8:9-11)

Simon was no match for the true man of God. Philip possessed what Simon only claimed to possess. Like the others, Simon believed and was baptized.

Even Simon himself believed, and after being baptized he continued with Philip. And seeing signs and great miracles performed, he was amazed (Acts 8:13)

Simon was a common name. Two of the original twelve apostles were named Simon (Simon Peter and Simon the Zealot), Jesus had a brother named Simon, Judas Iscariot's father was named Simon, Jesus spent time in the homes of two Simons (Simon the Pharisee and Simon the leper), Simon of Cyrene helped carry the cross to Calvary, and Peter stayed with Simon the tanner in Joppa. Obviously the Simon in Acts 8 is different from those other Simons.

Human reasoning would disqualify a man like Simon before he even had a chance to hear the message. It would predetermine that he "isn't interested" or "won't change." Yet we see that the gospel message is powerful enough to prick any heart — even the heart of a fraud. Simon was saved! He went from amazing others to being amazed himself: "He had amazed them...he was amazed" (Acts 8:11, 13).

Simon has been the source of much controversy. Some deny that he was really saved since he was clearly in danger of losing his soul later in the chapter. Their denials, however, are without merit. There is no doubt that Simon was saved when he obeyed the gospel. (1) The Lord's statement in Mark 16:16 promised salvation to those who believed and were baptized. Simon did that. (2) The phrase "Even Simon himself believed" indicates that his belief was the same as the others in Samaria. If we deny that his belief was sincere, then the other Samaritans must not have been sincere either. (3) Simon was told to "repent...and pray" when he sinned later in the chapter. That is the second law of pardon for erring Christians. (4) Simon was told only to repent for the one sin just committed, not for all the sins of his past life. If he were never saved, he would need to repent of a whole lot more than just that one sin. (5) Some period of time lapsed before Simon sinned. This is proven by the phrase "he continued with Philip" and by the fact that the apostles in Jerusalem had time to receive the news and travel to Samaria before he sinned. Yet there is nothing said about Simon's character during all that time. He was recognized by Philip and the Samaritan believers as a faithful brother in Christ.

We all agree that Simon's sin was terrible, but so was Peter's sin in Galatians 2:11-14. The fact that someone sins doesn't mean he was never saved.

Simon proves that a Christian can so sin as to be lost. Without repentance, he would have perished. There are many examples in the New Testament of men and women who fell from grace: Ananias, Sapphira, Hymenaeus, Alexander, Philetus, Demas, and others. Consider the chart below.

Disciples	IF you abide in my word (John 8:31)
Saved	IF you hold fast to the word (1 Corinthians 15:1-2)
Reap	IF we do not give up (Galatians 6:9)
Holy	IF you continue in the faith (Colossians 1:22-23)
Never Fall	IF you practice these qualities (2 Peter 1:10)
Cleansed	IF we walk in the light (1 John 1:7)

ESV

Every honest person can see that there are conditions a child of God must meet and maintain to be saved. "If" is a conditional word!

Simon, who had called himself "great" (v. 9), now stood in amazement of something truly "great" (v. 13). He beheld the mighty miracles God worked through Philip. This is just one of the many word-plays in the book of Acts.

When news reached the apostles in Jerusalem that the Samaritans had obeyed the gospel, it was determined that Peter and John should go there to impart the miraculous gifts to them.

Now when the apostles at Jerusalem heard that Samaria had received the word of God, they sent to them Peter and John, who came down and prayed for them that they might receive the Holy Spirit, for he had not yet fallen on any of them, but they had only been baptized in the name of the Lord Jesus. Then they laid their hands on them and they received the Holy Spirit (Acts 8:14-17)

Peter and John were close companions (Acts 3:1; 4:19; Galatians 2:9). It is not surprising then that they made this trip together. The fact that they were "sent" by the other apostles shows that no apostle was above the others in authority.

As noted before, the miraculous gifts were imparted by the laying on of the apostles' hands. That is why it was necessary for Peter and John to travel the distance from Jerusalem to Samaria. Since the apostles are no longer living, it should be understood that there are no miraculous gifts being imparted today. The gifts assisted the early church in the proclamation and preservation of the truth until it was fully made known (New Testament completed). Although Philip could perform them, he could not impart them.

The phrase "laid their hands on them" in this passage was the means by which the miraculous gifts were imparted (Acts 19:6). The phrase is not always used that way, however. It can also mean to arrest (Acts 4:3, KJV), to commend (Acts 13:3), or to heal (Luke 13:13).

John was one of the original twelve apostles, and part of the Lord's inner circle (Matthew 17:1; Mark 5:37; 13:3; 14:33). His brother James was also an apostle. His parents were named Zebedee and Salome. John was a fisherman by trade. He wrote one of the Gospels, three epistles, and the book of Revelation. He lived longer than any other apostle.

In addition to being part of the Lord's inner circle, which also included Peter and James, he was granted the privilege of sitting next to the Lord at the Last Supper and caring for his mother. He is even referred to as "the disciple whom Jesus loved" (John 13:23; 20:2; 21:7, 20).

It is likely that John's mother Salome and Mary were sisters. If so, that would make John and Jesus cousins, which would also mean that John was related to John the baptizer.

It is interesting to note that John was one of the men selected to travel to Samaria because he was one of the disciples who asked Jesus if he should call down fire from heaven on the Samaritans when they refused to provide lodging for them during the Lord's earthly ministry

(Luke 9:52-56). That incident may shed some light on why John and his brother James were nicknamed "Sons of Thunder" (Mark 3:17). Apparently they had a fiery temperament at times. Now, however, we see John acting more like his other nickname — the apostle of love. He went with Peter to help the Samaritans.

When Simon saw that it was possible for the gifts to be imparted, he fell into temptation and sinned. He wanted that power! This is not much different than what we see today — babes in Christ falling into the sins that controlled their lives before they were converted.

Now when Simon saw that the Spirit was given through the laying on of the apostles' hands, he offered them money, saying, "Give me this power also, so that anyone on whom I lay my hands may receive the Holy Spirit" (Acts 8:18-19)

Nothing God offers can be purchased with money. Simon was carnally minded and covetous. His request was an insult to the Spirit of God and to the apostles of Christ. Therefore, Peter was blunt in his rebuke of this new convert.

But Peter said to him, "May your silver perish with you, because you thought you could obtain the gift of God with money! You have neither part nor lot in this matter, for your heart is not right before God. Repent, therefore, of this wickedness of yours, and pray to the Lord that, if possible, the intent of your heart may be forgiven you. For I see that you are in the gall of bitterness and in the bond of iniquity" (Acts 8:20-23)

Simon was terrified to hear that he had done such a terrible thing, and he asked Peter to pray for him (James 5:16-20). He no doubt made that request because of the apostles' favor with God.

And Simon answered, "Pray for me to the Lord, that nothing of what you have said may come upon me" (Acts 8:24)

Simon's response indicates that he was sincere. He humbly asked for help in making things right with God. Nothing in this chapter, including his response to Peter's rebuke, suggests that Simon's faith was superficial.

Peter and John finished their work among the new believers and made their way back to Jerusalem. Along the way, they took time to proclaim the message in many of the Samaritan villages. This practice was echoed by Philip later in Acts 8 as he traveled to Caesarea (v. 40). The book of Acts does not mention any more of John's activities after this point. We do know from Galatians 2:9, however, that he was present at the Jerusalem meeting in Acts 15. Peter next appears in Acts 9:32.

During his earthly ministry, Jesus was filled with goodwill toward the Samaritans. He shared the message of hope with them as he passed through their land (John 4:4-30), healed a Samaritan of leprosy (Luke 17:16), and made a Samaritan the hero of one of his most famous parables (Luke 10:30-37). Now we see a church established in Samaria!

Review

Disciples scattered from Jerusalem

Philip proclaimed message in Samaria

Samaritans believed and were baptized

Simon, a magician, believed and was baptized

Two apostles came and imparted miraculous gifts

CHAPTER 3

THE ETHIOPIAN EUNUCH

Having established a church in Samaria, Philip was visited by an angel of the Lord and given a new task. There was fruit to reap in the desert!

Now an angel of the Lord said to Philip, "Rise and go toward the south to the road that goes down from Jerusalem to Gaza." This is a desert place (Acts 8:26)

We frequently read about angels in the book of Acts. It should be noted, however, that an angel never proclaimed the gospel message to lost sinners. Men were responsible for that work (2 Corinthians 4:7). The angel called upon Philip to proclaim the message.

The reference to the area being "a desert place" doesn't mean that it was waterless. It simply means that it was uninhabited. The fact that the eunuch was immersed in water later in the chapter proves that there were bodies of water in the area.

When Philip arrived at the designated spot, he observed a chariot passing by carrying a eunuch from Ethiopia. He was then instructed by the Spirit to join it.

And he rose and went. And there was an Ethiopian, a eunuch, a court official of Candace, queen of the Ethiopians, who was in charge of all her treasure. He had come to Jerusalem to worship and

was returning, seated in his chariot, and he was reading the prophet Isaiah. And the Spirit said to Philip, "Go over and join this chariot" (Acts 8:27-29)

Philip sets a great example of obedience by immediately doing what he was told to do. He did not argue or try to rationalize the command in his own mind before obeying it. He just "rose and went."

Eunuchs were emasculated men who were rendered impotent. They were commonly employed as court officials in the Near East. This particular eunuch was the treasurer of Ethiopia, which was a very high-ranking office. "Candace" was the title given to all of the queens of Ethiopia, just as "Pharaoh" was the title given to all of the kings of Egypt and "Caesar" was the title given to all of the emperors of Rome. Ethiopia was a large kingdom located south of Egypt on the Nile River, north of the land known as Ethiopia today.

The eunuch was returning from worship in Jerusalem, although his condition would prevent him from fully participating in the worship (Deuteronomy 23:1). This indicates that the eunuch was a dedicated proselyte.

The eunuch's chariot was larger than a military carriage, for it could hold at least three people — the driver, the eunuch, and Philip. As Philip approached the chariot, he heard the eunuch reading aloud from the prophet Isaiah. It was customary in those days for people to read out loud. Philip initiated the conversation with a question.

So Philip ran to him and heard him reading Isaiah the

**prophet and asked, "Do you understand what you are reading?"
(Acts 8:30)**

The chariot was moving slowly enough to allow for reading and for Philip to approach it on foot. The fact that the eunuch could give his attention to reading and that he later *commands* the chariot to stop indicates he had a driver.

Many today would be offended if a total stranger ran up to them as they were reading and asked, "Do you understand what you are reading?" The eunuch, however, was not offended. He humbly admitted the difficulty he was having with the passage and asked the stranger to come aboard.

And he said, "How can I, unless someone guides me?" And he invited Philip to come up and sit with him (Acts 8:31)

There is a difference between reading scripture and actually understanding it (Acts 13:27). The eunuch was reading the words of Isaiah, but he could not understand the meaning of those words. Therefore, he asked the stranger for help. It should also be noted that Philip was knowledgeable enough in the scriptures to help the eunuch. One can't teach others if he doesn't know himself (1 Peter 3:15)!

The eunuch was a man of great integrity. His character was exemplary. This is clearly seen from the context. (1) He had gained the confidence of the queen. She would not appoint a man lacking integrity to such an important office. (2) He traveled a long distance in a slow-moving chariot to worship in Jerusalem. The rough, uncomfortable ride did not hinder him from trying to serve God. (3) He took time away from his job to fulfill his religious obligations. His religion was more important than his work. (4) On his way home from worship, he was still reading the scriptures. (5) He was not offended when Philip asked him if he understood what he was reading.

The fact that the eunuch was not offended when Philip, a stranger, asked him if he understood what he was reading is remarkable. Such humility is hard to find, especially among those who hold high positions in government. He was not too proud to admit he needed help understanding the prophet.

Although the eunuch was a man of great integrity, he still needed to hear the gospel message and obey it. This proves that goodness alone will not save. Even the most morally-sound people still need Jesus!

After entering the chariot, the eunuch questioned Philip about the text in Isaiah, which just happened to be a messianic prophecy.

Now the passage of the Scripture that he was reading was this: "Like a sheep he was led to the slaughter and like a lamb before its shearer is silent, so he opens not his mouth. In his humiliation justice was denied him. Who can describe his generation? For his life is taken away from the earth." And the eunuch said to Philip, "About whom, I ask you, does the prophet say this, about himself or about someone else?" (Acts 8:32-34)

The eunuch was reading from the Septuagint (LXX), which was a Greek translation of the Hebrew scriptures. Jesus and the apostles often quoted from the Septuagint in the New Testament. The text was Isaiah 53:7-8, which was one of the great "Servant" passages.

The eunuch's question was often debated among the Jews. Some felt that the slaughtered sheep represented the prophet himself, others the nation, and still others the coming Messiah. Although Isaiah suffered martyrdom, being sawn asunder according to Jewish history, the text in Isaiah 53 was not about him. Nor was it about the nation. It had reference to the coming Messiah — Jesus of Nazareth! Philip then told the eunuch about him.

Then Philip opened his mouth, and beginning with this Scripture he told him the good news about Jesus (Acts 8:35)

One could hardly find a better text for such a situation. Using the prophecy of the suffering Messiah as a starting point, Philip preached the gospel message to the eunuch. He no doubt mentioned the miraculous birth in Bethlehem (Isaiah 7:14), the forerunner who prepared the way (Isaiah 40:3), the betrayal of Judas Iscariot (Psalm 41:9), the crucifixion between two thieves (Isaiah 53:12), and the glorious resurrection (Psalm 16:10). It was a message the eunuch had been longing to hear!

We should emphasize again that the gospel message has been left in human hands. Why did the angel commission Philip to proclaim the message to the eunuch rather than just doing it himself? He commissioned Philip because the responsibility of proclaiming the message has been given to men, not angels.

Philip's preaching must have mentioned the necessity of

baptism since the eunuch asked what stopped him from it. He was eager to be immersed!

And as they were going along the road they came to some water, and the eunuch said, "See, here is water! What prevents me from being baptized?" (Acts 8:36)

As noted in chapter 1 of this book, one contacts the blood of Christ when he is baptized in water. It is not until baptism that his sins are forgiven (Acts 2:38; 22:16). It is no wonder then that the eunuch demanded to know what prevented him from being baptized. He wanted to be "born again" (John 3:3).

Those familiar with the King James Version (KJV) may notice that newer versions of the Bible do not include verse 37. That is because it does not appear in any of the most ancient Greek manuscripts. This is not to say, however, that the eunuch did not confess his faith in Jesus Christ as the Son of God. There is no doubt that he did. Many other passages state that confession is necessary for salvation (Romans 10:9-10; 1 Timothy 6:12).

Having confessed his faith in Jesus Christ, nothing stopped the eunuch from being baptized.

And he commanded the chariot to stop, and they both went down into the water, Philip and the eunuch, and he baptized him. And when they came up out of the water, the Spirit of the Lord carried Philip away, and the eunuch saw him no more, and went on his way rejoicing (Acts 8:38-39)

The eunuch commanded the chariot to stop and rendered his obedience to the gospel message. Like the Jews and Samaritans, his sins were washed away by the blood of Christ!

The Greek word "baptized" *(ebaptisen)* means to immerse or to dip. Sprinkling and pouring for baptism was unknown in the New Testament. Baptism was always a burial in water (Romans 6:3-5; Colossians 2:12-13). That is why the text says they "went down" into the water and "came up."

Was it just coincidence that Philip and the eunuch crossed paths? Was it just coincidence that the eunuch was reading from Isaiah 53, which just happens to be a messianic prophecy, when Philip approached? Was it just coincidence that there was a body of water nearby when the eunuch was ready to be baptized? These things were not coincidental, but providential.

Having been raised to walk in newness of life, the eunuch got back into his chariot and continued home rejoicing. He knew the Savior! His sins were gone! We should also note that rejoicing occurred *after* baptism in the book of Acts (Acts 16:34).

Philip was taken away from the eunuch in a miraculous way. The words "carried away" *(herpasen)* mean to catch away or to snatch up. The same word is used in reference to Paul being caught up to the third heaven (2 Corinthians 12:2-4) and living saints being caught up at the Second Coming (1 Thessalonians 4:17). The word is not always used in a miraculous sense, however (Acts 23:10). Philip was dropped off in a town about 20 miles north of Gaza called Azotus.

But Philip found himself at Azotus, and as he passed through he preached the gospel to all the towns until he came to Caesarea (Acts 8:40)

Azotus, which was once the ancient Philistine city of Ashdod, was on the main coastal road leading from Gaza to Joppa. The city is mentioned only here in the New Testament. Just as Peter and John preached in every village as they returned to Jerusalem (Acts 8:25), Philip preached in every village on his way to Caesarea, which was about 60 miles from Azotus. Philip apparently made his home in Caesarea because he was living there with his family twenty years later when Paul came to visit. By that time, Philip had four daughters, each of whom had the gift of prophecy (Acts 21:8-9). As for the eunuch, nothing more is said about him in the New Testament. Irenaeus says that he became a missionary in Ethiopia.

Review
Philip dispatched to desert
Philip met eunuch from Ethiopia
Philip proclaimed message to eunuch
Eunuch confessed his faith and was baptized
Eunuch returned home rejoicing

CHAPTER 4

SAUL OF TARSUS

Saul was born in Tarsus of Cilicia. Tarsus was a great commercial center, educational center, and the capital of the province. Although he was a Roman citizen by birth, Saul was from the tribe of Benjamin and had strong Jewish roots. He was circumcised the eighth day and sat at the feet of the famous rabbi Gamaliel in Jerusalem (Acts 22:3; Philippians 3:5-6). His religious zeal allowed him to advance above others his own age (Galatians 1:14). Saul was a tentmaker by trade.

We are first introduced to Saul at the stoning of Stephen. Stephen was a disciple of Christ who was put to death for preaching the gospel message (see chapter 2). In Saul's eyes, however, he was a heretic and blasphemer. Therefore, Saul approved of the actions taken against him.

Then they cast him out of the city and stoned him. And the witnesses laid down their garments at the feet of a young man named Saul...And Saul approved of his execution (Acts 7:58; 8:1a)

After the death of Stephen, Saul was emboldened. He initiated a campaign of intense persecution against the disciples, pursuing and imprisoning them. His hostility was unmistakable.

But Saul was ravaging the church, and entering house after house, he dragged off men and women and committed them to prison (Acts 8:3)

The word "ravaging" *(elymaineto)* means to ruin or to damage. The idea is that of a wild beast tearing at raw flesh. This is the only time the word appears in the New Testament. It was not until after his conversion that the churches again had "peace" for a time (9:31). Ironically, the one dragging and imprisoning would one day be dragged and imprisoned himself (16:19-23).

By Acts 9, Saul was so determined to rid the world of Christianity that he received permission from the high priest to broaden his pursuit of the disciples to Damascus. The high priest served as head of the Sanhedrin, which was the Jewish legislative body. Caiaphas was high priest at the time. He was the son-in-law of Annas (John 18:13).

But Saul, still breathing threats and murder against the disciples of the Lord, went to the high priest and asked him for letters to the synagogues at Damascus, so that if he found any belonging to the Way, men or women, he might bring them bound to Jerusalem (Acts 9:1-2)

Damascus, which was the ancient capital of Syria, was one of the ten cities in the region known as the "Decapolis" (Mark 5:20). It was a thriving commercial center situated at the intersection of important trade routes. Damascus had a large Jewish population, which is evidenced by the fact that there were several synagogues there (9:2), and Josephus states that no fewer than 10,000 Jews were killed at the time of the Jewish revolt against Rome in A. D. 66. The large Jewish presence may be why Saul chose Damascus.

Saul was convinced that those belonging to the Way were

enemies of God and needed to be crushed. Therefore, he pursued them "in raging fury" (26:11). His actions, however, made him the true enemy of God. "The Way" is an expression used throughout the book of Acts referring to Christianity (9:2; 19:9, 23; 22:4; 24:14, 22; Isaiah 35:8). This was one of the earliest designations for the church. The familiar term "Christian" did not appear until Acts 11 in Antioch (v. 26). The term appears two other times in the New Testament (26:28; 1 Peter 4:16).

Having received permission from the high priest, Saul and his companions made their way toward Damascus, which was about 140 miles away. Although we are not told the method of travel they used in making this journey, the fact that Saul's companions later "led him by the hand" into the city probably means they were on foot. The journey would take nearly a week to complete. Along the way, Saul met Jesus!

Now as he went on his way, he approached Damascus, and suddenly a light from heaven flashed around him. And falling to the ground he heard a voice saying to him, "Saul, Saul, why are you persecuting me?" And he said, "Who are you, Lord?" And he said, "I am Jesus, whom you are persecuting. But rise and enter the city, and you will be told what you are to do" (Acts 9:3-6)

The light that flashed around Saul was "brighter than the sun" (26:13) and forced him and his companions to the ground. It was not uncommon for a bright light to accompany a heavenly encounter (Luke 2:9; 9:29; Acts 12:7). He then heard a voice in the Hebrew language (Aramaic—NIV, 26:14) calling his name. There are several times in the gospels where Jesus repeated a name. He said, "Martha,

Martha" (Luke 10:41), "Jerusalem, Jerusalem" (Luke 13:34), and "Simon, Simon" (Luke 22:31). In each instance, the name is repeated to indicate deep emotion. The same is true here. Saul's name was repeated out of deep emotion. The double calling of a name is also found in the Old Testament (Genesis 22:11; 46:2; Exodus 3:4; 1 Samuel 3:10). Saul was awe-struck!

Saul must have been terrified to hear the speaker identify himself as "Jesus, whom you are persecuting." At that moment, he knew that Jesus of Nazareth was alive, that Stephen had told the truth, and that he, not the disciples, was the enemy of God. Gamaliel's worst fears had come to pass (Acts 5:39). Saul was then led into the city where he would be told what he must do.

The scriptures are clear that Saul *saw* the Lord during the Damascus road encounter. Jesus appeared to the persecutor (9:17, 27; 22:14; 26:16; 1 Corinthians 9:1; 15:8). It was both an audible and visible experience. Interestingly, the last person to see the glorified Christ before Saul was Stephen! This is the first of six recorded visions that Saul (Paul) received in the book of Acts (9:3-12; 16:9-10; 18:9-10; 22:17-21; 23:11; 27:23-24).

Those familiar with the King James Version (KJV) may notice that newer versions of the Bible do not include the phrase "it is hard for thee to kick against the pricks" in verse 5. That is because it does not appear in any of the most ancient Greek manuscripts. The phrase was no doubt added later from 26:14, where the phrase is genuine.

Some believe that Saul was converted on the road to Damascus because he refers to Jesus as "Lord." However, Saul did not even know that it was Jesus at that point. Therefore, we must understand "Lord" as simply a courteous title, much like our word "sir" today. Saul was not forgiven of his sins until baptism (22:16).

Although Saul was wrong for persecuting the church, we should note that he acted "in all good conscience" (23:1) and "was convinced" (26:9) that it was the will of God. That is exactly the type of situation Jesus had in mind when he told the disciples, "They will put you out of the synagogues. Indeed, the hour is coming when whoever kills you will think he is offering service to God" (John 16:2). Saul was sincere, but sincerely wrong!

We should also note the relationship that exists between Christ and the church. The two are inseparable (Matthew 25:35-45). When they are rejected, he is rejected (Luke 10:16). That is because the church is the body of Christ (Colossians 1:18). By persecuting the church (Galatians 1:13), Saul was persecuting the Lord himself. The union between Christ and the church would later become a vital part of Saul's teaching.

Saul entered Damascus much different than he anticipated. Instead of triumphantly entering the city with his chin up and chest out, he was helplessly led by the hand because the encounter left him blind. Since his companions also saw the light (22:9), it must have been the brightness of the glorified Christ, which only Saul witnessed, that left him blind.

Saul rose from the ground, and although his eyes were opened, he saw nothing. So they led him by the hand and brought

him into Damascus. And for three days he was without sight, and neither ate nor drank (Acts 9:8-9)

There is great significance to the fact that Saul was accompanied by others in this account. They were witnesses to the encounter. Although they did not understand what was being said or actually see Jesus, they did experience the jolt of the bright light. Therefore, they could testify that Saul's experience that day was an objective one. He had not lost his mind; something extraordinary really happened along the way.

We also have more proof that Saul was not yet saved from his sins. Salvation resulted in great joy in the book of Acts (8:39; 16:34). Saul, however, was anything but happy at this point. He couldn't see and wouldn't eat. If he were saved on the road to Damascus, he was the most pitiful saved person to ever live!

While Saul waited in Damascus, the Lord commissioned a disciple named Ananias to visit him. Ananias was a common name. In fact, three men have this name in the book of Acts. The other two men were Ananias the hypocrite (5:1) and Ananias the high priest (23:2). The Ananias who the Lord commissioned to visit Saul was "a devout man according to the law, well spoken of by all the Jews" (22:12). The commission must have come as quite a shock!

Now there was a disciple at Damascus named Ananias. The Lord said to him in a vision, "Ananias." And he said, "Here I am, Lord." And the Lord said to him, "Rise and go to the street called Straight, and at the house of Judas look for a man of Tarsus named Saul, for behold, he is praying, and he has seen in a vision a man

named Ananias come in and lay hands on him so that he might regain his sight" (Acts 9:10-12)

Both Saul and Ananias received visions from the Lord in which he called them by name. In Acts 10, Cornelius received a vision in which an angel of God called him by name (v. 3). It is awesome to know that God knows us by name!

While the Lord was conversing with Ananias, Saul was praying. What do you suppose he was praying for? Forgiveness! There is no doubt that he spent those hours on his knees begging God for forgiveness. Yet he was not forgiven of his sins until baptism (22:16). This proves that the "sinner's prayer" is unscriptural. No one in the book of Acts was converted to Christ through prayer.

Saul went from "breathing threats and murder" (9:1) to "praying" (9:11). His harshness was replaced with humility!

Saul of Tarsus was staying on Straight Street at Judas' house. Straight Street, which ran east to west with colonnades on both sides, was the major road in the city. Like the name Ananias, Judas was a common name. In fact, two of the original twelve apostles were named Judas (Judas the son of James and Judas Iscariot). Saul had probably made arrangements to stay with Judas prior to leaving Jerusalem. At first, Ananias was reluctant to go see Saul. His hesitation was the result of the persecutor's fierce reputation. It would be like asking a Jew to visit Hitler!

But Ananias answered, "Lord, I have heard from many about this man, how much evil he has done to your saints at Jerusalem.

And here he has authority from the chief priests to bind all who call on your name" (Acts 9:13-14)

The disciples in Damascus had been warned that Saul was on his way to their city with the authority to arrest Christians. This struck fear in Ananias. The fact that Ananias had only "heard" of the evil done to the saints in Jerusalem indicates that he had not been in Jerusalem during the persecution, but had received the information from others.

It is important to note that living Christians were called "saints" in verse 13. This is very different from the Roman Catholic teaching that only the deceased can be canonized into sainthood. The scriptures teach that *all* Christians are saints. This passage marks the first time that disciples are called saints in the book of Acts (9:32, 41; 26:10). The term denotes those who have been sanctified by the blood of Christ through their obedience to the gospel message. They are the holy ones, having been consecrated to God's service.

When Moses was reluctant to approach Pharaoh and lead the people out of Egyptian bondage, the Lord offered words of assurance to him (Exodus 3:11-12). We see the same thing here. The Lord reassured the reluctant disciple that the man who had done much to destroy the church would now do much to advance it. He was a chosen instrument.

But the Lord said to him, "Go, for he is a chosen instrument of mine to carry my name before the Gentiles and kings and the children of Israel. For I will show him how much he must suffer for the sake of my name" (Acts 9:15-16)

The Lord had a plan for Saul. The persecutor would soon carry his name among the Gentiles, which was his primary calling (Romans 11:13; 15:16; Galatians 1:16; 2:8; 1 Timothy 2:7; 2 Timothy 1:11). He would also carry it before kings and the children of Israel. The one who had inflicted much suffering upon the disciples would experience much suffering himself!

Although his primary calling was to the Gentiles, Saul would practice a "Jew-first" form of evangelism throughout the book of Acts (13:5, 14, 46; 14:1; 16:13; 17:1, 10, 17; 18:4, 19; 19:8; 28:23-28). Upon hearing what the Lord had in store for the persecutor, Ananias went to see Saul.

So Ananias departed and entered the house. And laying hands on him he said, "Brother Saul, the Lord Jesus who appeared to you on the road by which you came has sent me so that you may regain your sight and be filled with the Holy Spirit" (Acts 9:17)

One can only imagine how Ananias felt as he made his way down Straight Street to the designated house. It must have been similar to the way Moses felt as he approached Pharaoh or to the way Elijah felt as he approached Ahab. What faith!

Saul had intended to go looking for men like Ananias when he arrived in Damascus. Now, however, it was Ananias that came looking for Saul.

Upon entering the house, Ananias laid hands on Saul and restored his sight. This indicates that at some point Ananias had received the laying on of the apostles' hands. Like Philip, he could perform the miraculous gifts, but not impart them to others. It is important to note that Saul saw more light during those days in darkness than he had ever seen before!

Ananias' use of the term "brother" has caused some to think that Saul was already saved at this point. Such is not the case, however, for he was not forgiven of his sins until baptism (22:16). Ananias called Saul his brother because they were Jewish brethren according to the flesh, not because they were Christian brethren according to the Spirit. Throughout the book of Acts we see examples of people calling one another brethren in this way (2:29, 37; 3:17; 7:2; 22:1). In Romans 9, Paul laments the unbelief of the Jews saying, "For I could wish that I myself were accursed and cut off from Christ for the sake of *my brothers*, my kinsmen according to the flesh" (v. 3, emphasis mine). So the term did not necessarily imply spiritual fellowship.

Despite the fact that he had been praying for three days (9:11), Saul was still in his sins and needed to be baptized. Therefore, Ananias told him exactly what he must do.

And now why do you wait? Rise and be baptized and wash away your sins, calling on his name (Acts 22:16)

One contacts the blood of Christ and has his sins forgiven when he is baptized in water (2:38). That is why we see such urgency in the words of Ananias: "Why do you wait?" (ESV) — "Why tarriest thou?" (KJV) — "Why wait any longer?" (NCV) — "What are you waiting for?" (NIV) — "Why do you delay?" (NRSV). Baptism is not to be delayed or postponed. It is to be done immediately. Saul wasted no time rendering his obedience to the gospel message.

Then he rose and was baptized (Acts 9:18b)

Although Saul had not eaten for several days (9:9), he went to be baptized before satisfying his appetite. This shows the importance of baptism. His soul was more important than his belly! Although the place of the baptism is not mentioned, it probably took place in the Abana River, which ran through the city.

What a privilege it must have been for Ananias to baptize Saul into Christ (Galatians 3:27). Such a privilege ranks right up there next to Moses leading the children of Israel out of Egypt or Peter unveiling the plan of salvation on Pentecost.

This remarkable episode, beginning on the Damascus road and concluding with Saul becoming a Christian a few days later, was frequently rehearsed in the book of Acts (22:4-16; 26:9-18). It was a life-changing and soul-shaking event that redirected Saul's focus forever. He went from sinner to saint, from persecutor to preacher, from murderer to martyr!

After obeying the gospel, Saul joined himself to the disciples in Damascus and went to work proclaiming the message. He wasted no time trying to make up for the damage he had done.

For some days he was with the disciples at Damascus. And immediately he proclaimed Jesus in the synagogues, saying, "He is the Son of God" (Acts 9:19-20)

Wow! The very synagogues he planned to visit in hopes of arresting Christians were now the places he went to proclaim the Christ. His zeal for Judaism was transformed into a zeal for Jesus! Better known to us as Paul the apostle (13:9), he would go on to write nearly half of the New Testament and establish countless churches. He never did forget his past, however (1 Corinthians 15:9; Galatians 1:13, 23; Philippians 3:6; 1 Timothy 1:13). Interestingly, this is the only time the title "Son of God" appears in Acts.

Proclaiming Christ in Jewish synagogues would become a common practice for Paul (13:5, 14; 14:1; 17:1-2, 10, 17; 18:4, 19; 19:8). This was an expedient way to take the gospel message to the Jews.

One final note is in order. We were first introduced to Saul at the stoning of Stephen. Ironically, Saul too would be stoned (although he did not die). When his martyrdom did finally arrive, he could write with confidence: "I have fought the good fight, I have finished the race, I have kept the faith. Henceforth there is laid up for me the crown of righteousness, which the Lord, the righteous judge, will award to me on that Day, and not only to me but also to all who have loved his appearing" (2 Timothy 4:7-8).

Review

Saul traveled to Damascus to persecute Christians

Jesus appeared to Saul on road to Damascus

Ananias dispatched to tell Saul how to be saved

Saul baptized to wash away sins

Saul proclaimed message in synagogues

CHAPTER 5

CORNELIUS

It was God's plan for all men to be saved — both Jew and Gentile. Just before his ascension into heaven, Jesus told the apostles that they would be his witnesses "in Jerusalem and in all Judea and Samaria, and to the end of the earth" (Acts 1:8). It was now time to bring the plan full circle.

Acts 10 is a monumental chapter in the book of Acts. It records the inclusion of uncircumcised Gentiles into the kingdom of God. The amount of space devoted to this account, which is more than the amount devoted to Pentecost, testifies to its importance.

There was a man in Caesarea named Cornelius. He served in the Roman military and feared God, although he was not a Jewish proselyte.

At Caesarea there was a man named Cornelius, a centurion of what was known as the Italian Cohort, a devout man who feared God with all his household, gave alms generously to the people, and prayed continually to God (Acts 10:1-2)

Caesarea was the Roman capital of Judea. It was built about 10 years before the birth of Christ by Herod the Great in honor of Caesar Augustus. It was situated on the Mediterranean coast about 65 miles northwest of Jerusalem. A "centurion" was a non-commissioned officer in the Roman military who commanded a unit of 100 soldiers.

A "cohort" was a group of 600 soldiers, though the number could vary. Just like every other centurion mentioned in the New Testament, Cornelius was spoken of in a favorable way.

Although he was never converted to Judaism through circumcision (Acts 11:3), Cornelius was a pious man who reverenced God. He was charitable and prayerful. His reputation was impeccable. It is no wonder then that he found divine favor and was given an opportunity to hear the gospel message.

About the ninth hour of the day he saw clearly in a vision an angel of God come in and say to him, "Cornelius." And he stared at him in terror and said, "What is it, Lord?" And he said to him, "Your prayers and your alms have ascended as a memorial before God. And now send men to Joppa and bring one Simon who is called Peter. He is lodging with one Simon, a tanner, whose house is by the seaside" (Acts 10:3-6)

The ninth hour (3:00pm) was one of the customary times for prayer among the Jews (Acts 3:1). It was at this time that Cornelius received the angelic vision. The angel appeared as a man in bright clothing (v. 30) and called him by name. The angel told Cornelius that his prayers and alms had risen like a sweet smelling sacrifice to God (Philippians 4:18) and that he needed to send for Peter in Joppa. Joppa was a coastal city located about 30 miles south of Caesarea. It was there that a disciple named Tabitha was raised from the dead (Acts 9:36-41). Peter would tell Cornelius how to be saved (11:14).

The fact that Peter was staying with a tanner shows that he had already shed some of his Jewish hang-ups because tanners were ceremonially unclean due to their frequent contact with dead animals. Peter still had some hang-ups, however, as we shall soon see.

Cornelius wasted no time fetching the preacher. He dispatched three loyal men to find Peter in Joppa.

When the angel who spoke to him had departed, he called two of his servants and a devout soldier from among those who attended to him, and having related everything to them, he sent them to Joppa (Acts 10:7-8)

As the three men made their way to Joppa, God prepared Peter for the visit by teaching him an important lesson about impartiality. He did this through a vision.

The next day, as they were on their journey and approaching the city, Peter went up on the housetop about the sixth hour to pray. And he became hungry and wanted something to eat, but while they were preparing it, he fell into a trance and saw the heavens opened and something like a great sheet descending, being let down by its four corners upon the earth. In it were all kinds of animals and reptiles and birds of the air. And there came a voice to him: "Rise, Peter; kill and eat." But Peter said, "By no means, Lord; for I have never eaten anything that is common or unclean." And the voice came to him again a second time, "What God has made clean, do not call common." This happened three times, and the thing was taken up at once to heaven (Acts 10:9-16)

Houses in Palestine were usually built with flat roofs that were accessible through outside stairways. At about the sixth hour (noon), Peter went upon the roof to pray when he fell into a trance. The word "trance" *(ekstasis)* means to stand out of oneself. It is from this word that we get our English word "ecstasy." This trance made Peter susceptible only to the vision.

The vision was like that of a great sheet descending from heaven with both clean and unclean animals in it. Peter then heard a voice ordering him to eat the animals, without making any distinctions, which was strictly forbidden under the Old Law (Leviticus 11). Despite Peter's protest, the voice ordered him to eat the animals three times. This was designed to teach Peter that Gentiles were acceptable candidates for the gospel (Acts 10:28) and that the Old Law, including its dietary restrictions, was no longer binding. As Peter thought about what he had seen, the three men from Caesarea arrived at the house. This is another example of God working providentially.

Now while Peter was inwardly perplexed as to what the vision that he had seen might mean, behold, the men who were sent by Cornelius, having made inquiry for Simon's house, stood at the gate and called out to ask whether Simon who was called Peter was lodging there (Acts 10:17-18)

Peter was told by the men that an angel directed Cornelius to send for him, and that he was to come proclaim the gospel message to the Gentiles. Peter then invited the men to spend the night before making the trip to Caesarea the next day. Six Jewish brothers accompanied Peter on the trip (Acts 10:23; 11:12).

When Peter arrived in Caesarea, he saw that many had come together to hear the message. Cornelius had been busy inviting others to share in the moment.

And on the following day they entered Caesarea. Cornelius was expecting them and had called together his relatives and close friends (Acts 10:24)

As Peter spoke, the Holy Spirit fell on the Gentiles in a remarkable display of God's grace.

While Peter was still saying these things, the Holy Spirit fell on all who heard the word. And the believers from among the circumcised who had come with Peter were amazed, because the gift of the Holy Spirit was poured out even on the Gentiles. For they were hearing them speaking in tongues and extolling God (Acts 10:44-46)

Holy Spirit baptism was not a regular occurrence. In fact, there is only one other recorded instance of it in the book of Acts (2:4). That is why Peter had to refer all the way back to "the beginning" for another example of it (Acts 11:15). The reason the Gentiles received Holy Spirit baptism on this occasion was to validate their acceptance with God. It bore witness to the Jews that Gentiles could be saved (Acts 15:8).

Many assume that Cornelius and the others were saved the moment they received Holy Spirit baptism. Not so. The text says they were to be saved by hearing the "message" (11:14). However, the Holy

Spirit fell as Peter "began to speak" (11:15). They had not even heard the message by which they would be saved yet!

As noted in the other conversions, upon hearing the gospel message one must be immersed in water to be forgiven of sins (Acts 2:38; 22:16). Therefore, Cornelius and the others were immediately baptized.

And he commanded them to be baptized in the name of Jesus Christ (Acts 10:48a)

How anyone can say that baptism is "unnecessary" or "optional" is incomprehensible. Here we have an apostle *commanding* someone to do it! That doesn't sound optional to me. After obeying the gospel, Cornelius insisted that Peter remain with them.

Then they asked him to remain for some days (Acts 10:48b)

What a great example of hospitality! Cornelius invited the apostle to stay in his home. One can assume that Peter accepted the invitation since the church at Jerusalem already knew of the Gentile conversions by the time he arrived there.

Peter first used the keys to unlock the doors of the kingdom for the Jews, now he used them to open the doors for the Gentiles as well. Things like race, rank, and nationality matter not to God. All those who hear and heed the message can be saved.

Cornelius was saved by grace (Acts 15:11). That was accomplished by hearing (10:33), believing (15:7), repenting (11:18), and being baptized (10:48). Salvation by grace is dependant upon an obedient faith.

Review
Gentile named Cornelius visited by angel
Cornelius sent for Simon Peter in Joppa
Cornelius filled with Spirit as Peter began to speak
Peter proclaimed message to Cornelius
Cornelius and his household were baptized

CHAPTER 6

LYDIA

Having been forbidden by the Holy Spirit to preach in Asia or Bithynia, Paul and his companions (Silas and Timothy) came to Troas. Troas was an important city in the western part of Mysia. While there, Paul received a vision of a man begging him to come to Macedonia. This vision is often called "The Macedonian Call."

And a vision appeared to Paul in the night: a man of Macedonia was standing there, urging him and saying, "Come over to Macedonia and help us" (Acts 16:9)

Macedonia was across the Aegean Sea from Troas. It was a Roman province and home to such cities as Philippi, Thessalonica, and Berea. Paul and his companions wasted no time answering the call. They boarded a ship and headed that way.

And when Paul had seen the vision, immediately we sought to go on into Macedonia, concluding that God had called us to preach the gospel to them (Acts 16:10)

This verse is the first of the "we" sections in the book of Acts (16:10-17; 20:5-21:18; 27:1-28:16), indicating that Luke joined the missionary team in Troas. The gospel coming to Macedonia is extremely significant. By sowing the seed of the gospel in cities along the Egnatian Way, it was sure to carry east into Asia and west toward

Rome. This was the second of six recorded visions Paul received in the book of Acts.

Perhaps we should take a moment to introduce the missionary team. Silas, also known as Silvanus, was a leading member of the Jerusalem church and was selected to accompany Paul and Barnabas as they delivered the letter from Jerusalem about circumcision to the church at Antioch (Acts 15:22). He was a prophet (Acts 15:32). Like Paul, Silas was a Roman citizen (Acts 16:37-38). He had the privilege of working with both Paul and Peter. Timothy was a young man from Lystra. His mother and grandmother had taught him the scriptures from childhood (2 Timothy 3:15) and instilled in him a deep respect for God. Timothy was probably converted to Christ by Paul since the apostle referred to Timothy as a "child" (1 Corinthians 4:17; 1 Timothy 1:2; 2 Timothy 1:2). Timothy's actual father was a Greek. Paul had so much confidence in Timothy that he often sent him to address concerns within the churches (1 Corinthians 4:17; Philippians 2:19; 1 Thessalonians 3:2; 1 Timothy 1:3). *He was Paul's troubleshooter!* We know that Timothy was imprisoned at least once for the sake of the gospel (Hebrews 13:23), and, according to tradition, was martyred in Ephesus. See Introduction for notes on Luke and Chapter 4 for notes on Paul.

The missionary team began their work in the city of Philippi. Philippi was located in eastern Macedonia about 10 miles inland from the Aegean Sea. The original settlement was named Krenides, but the name was changed to Philippi when the father of Alexander the Great, Philip II of Macedon, took control of it.

Philippi was the site of the decisive battle in which Antony and Octavian defeated Brutus and Cassius, the assassins of Julius Caesar (B. C. 42).

Philippi was a wealthy city, primarily because of its location along the Egnatian Way, which was the major east-west highway of the Roman Empire. The city was also famous for its school of medicine and agriculture.

It was Paul's custom in each city he visited to preach in the synagogue (13:5, 14; 14:1; 17:1-2, 10, 17; 18:4, 19; 19:8), but apparently Philippi did not have one. So the missionary team went to the riverside hoping to find Jews assembling there.

And on the Sabbath day we went outside the gate to the riverside, where we supposed there was a place of prayer, and we sat down and spoke to the women who had come together (Acts 16:13)

Before a city could have a synagogue, there had to be at least 10 Jewish males living there. Since Philippi did not meet that requirement, the remaining Jews (in this case all women) were worshipping by a riverside, which Jews would often do in the absence of a synagogue in order to perform their ceremonial washings. It is likely that these women were gathered on the banks of the Gangites River, which was located about 1 mile west of the city.

It was common for rabbis to sit down while teaching. In fact, it was only when a rabbi sat down that his words were considered authoritative and official. If he spoke while standing his words were considered informal and unofficial. Jesus often sat down to teach

(Matthew 5:1; 13:2; 23:2; John 8:2). Now we see Paul sitting down to teach as well.

The women were very receptive to the gospel message. They listened to the preaching of Paul and were obedient to it. This indicates that they were sincere in trying to do what was right. One of the women was named Lydia.

One who heard us was a woman named Lydia, from the city of Thyatira, a seller or purple goods, who was a worshiper of God. The Lord opened her heart to pay close attention to what was said by Paul. And after she was baptized, and her household as well, she urged us, saying, "If you have judged me to be faithful to the Lord, come to my house and stay." And she prevailed upon us (Acts 16:14-15)

Lydia was a seller of purple goods from Thyatira. Thyatira was a city in the province of Asia and a major manufacturer of purple dye in the first century. It was also home to one of the seven churches in Revelation (Revelation 2:18-29). Since the purple industry was quite prosperous, we can safely assume that Lydia was a wealthy woman. The fact that she had a house large enough to accommodate four visitors in addition to her own household gives even more support to that assumption (v. 15). Yet she did not allow her prosperity to keep her from being spiritually-minded.

We are told that the Lord "opened her heart." This phrase is often quoted by Calvinists to affirm their doctrine of the direct operation of the Holy Spirit upon the heart in producing faith. It teaches no such thing. Lydia had her heart opened by the Lord just like everyone else in the book of Acts — through the preaching of the gospel.

> Acts 2:37 — "Heard…cut to the heart"
> Acts 4:4 — "Heard...believed"
> Acts 14:1 — "Spoke…believed"
> Acts 18:8 — "Hearing…believed"

The idea that one cannot have faith until the direct operation of the Holy Spirit miraculously takes place upon his heart is absurd. The scriptures clearly teach that faith comes by hearing the gospel message (Romans 10:17). In fact, the consequences of such a doctrine are beyond comprehension. For instance, if a man cannot have faith until the Holy Spirit comes upon him, whose fault is it if he dies in unbelief? That would make it God's fault! Furthermore, if a man cannot have faith until the Holy Spirit comes upon him, why did Jesus marvel at unbelief (Mark 6:6)? Why did he command that the gospel be preached to every creature (Mark 16:15)? Why did Peter tell the Jews on Pentecost to save themselves (Acts 2:40)? Calvinism is false!

> Calvinism: Faith comes by direct operation of Holy Spirit
> New Testament: Faith comes by hearing Word of God
> (Romans 10:17)

As is the case with every detailed conversion in the book of Acts, Lydia and the others believed the message and were immediately baptized.

Some argue that Lydia's household included infants. This argument is made in hopes of proving that infant baptism is scriptural. However, there is absolutely no evidence that infants were baptized. One would have to assume that Lydia was married, had children, had *infant* children, and that her infant children were with her at the time of her conversion. It is much more likely that Lydia's household consisted of either employees or servants.

The fact that Lydia appears as the head of her household probably indicates that she was either unmarried or widowed.

After Lydia was baptized into Christ (Romans 6:3; Galatians 3:27), she urged Paul and his companions to stay in her home. Like Cornelius, she sets a great example of hospitality. The generous spirit of the first converts in Philippi would characterize the church there for years to come (Philippians 4:15-18). The missionary team remained in her home while in the city.

The conversion of Lydia and the others on the riverside marks the first-fruits of the Macedonian Call.

Review
Paul dispatched to Macedonia
Paul proclaimed message in Philippi
Lydia's heart opened by message
Lydia and her household were baptized
Paul and companions stayed in her home

CHAPTER 7

THE JAILER

After the conversion of Lydia and the others on the riverside, Paul and his companions remained in Philippi for some time proclaiming the message. It was not long, however, until they faced intense opposition.

Still meeting on the riverside, which is called the "place of prayer" by Luke, the group conducted their activities in peace until a demon-possessed slave girl started endorsing their work.

As we were going to the place of prayer, we were met by a slave girl who had a spirit of divination and brought her owners much gain by fortune-telling. She followed Paul and us, crying out, "These men are servants of the Most High God, who proclaim to you the way of salvation" (Acts 16:16-17)

The girl had a spirit of divination (lit: python). The phrase "Most High God" was also used by the demonic in Mark 5:7. Although her statement was true, it would not be good having someone demon-possessed endorsing your work. People may think that the missionaries and the demon were somehow united. Therefore, after many days of tolerating the shouts, Paul let out a shout of his own!

And this she kept doing for many days. Paul, having become greatly annoyed, turned and said to the spirit, "I command you in

the name of Jesus Christ to come out of her." And it came out that
very hour (Acts 16:18)

By divine authority, Paul commanded the demon to depart
from the girl. This undoubtedly brought her great relief from the pain
and suffering she had endured as a result of the possession. Yet her
owners were outraged! They exploited the demon possession for
financial gain and seeing that their money was gone, they angrily
dragged Paul and Silas before the city leaders.

But when her owners saw their hope of gain was gone, they
seized Paul and Silas and dragged them into the marketplace before
the rulers (Acts 16:19)

Instead of being grateful that the girl was comforted, all these
men could see was lost money. Their hearts were consumed by greed.
Therefore, they seized Paul and Silas and brought charges against
them in court. Interestingly, Paul, who dragged off Christians to face
punishment before his conversion (Acts 8:3) was now being dragged
off himself.

Acts 8:3 — "Saul...dragged off men and women"
Acts 16:19 — "Paul...dragged...into the marketplace"

This was not the first time that Paul had been "dragged" by an
angry mob (Acts 14:19), nor the last time (Acts 21:30). Other disciples
were also "dragged" in the book of Acts (17:6).

In that day men could do their own arresting. The marketplace
(agoran) was the town square, which served as the social center. It was

there that the unemployed waited for work, the sick were treated, and the magistrates heard court cases. The marketplace was bustling with people.

Everywhere Paul went there was either a riot or a revival. Philippi was no exception. The accusations against the missionaries struck a nerve with those standing nearby and sent them into such an uproar that the magistrates ordered Paul and Silas to be beaten and imprisoned.

The crowd joined in attacking them, and the magistrates tore the garments off them and gave orders to beat them with rods. And when they had inflicted many blows upon them, they threw them into prison, ordering the jailer to keep them safely (Acts 16:22-23)

Unlike the Jews who used a leather whip and were limited to 40 stripes, the Romans used a rod and had no limits as to the number of blows one could receive. Therefore, it is impossible to know just how severe the beating may have been. Were they beaten 40 times? 50 times? 60 times? All the text says is that they received "many blows." This beating left their bodies lacerated and bleeding.

Roman beatings were sometimes fatal. Cicero gives an account of a man named Gaius Servilius who was beaten to death. Paul suffered this punishment from the Romans at least three times (2 Corinthians 11:25) and bore the marks on his body to prove it (Galatians 6:17).

As Roman citizens, Paul and Silas should have never been beaten with rods because it was illegal. The Valerian and Porcian laws expressly stated that Roman citizens were not to be beaten.

Nonetheless, they were tied to a pole, stripped from their waist up, and brutally beaten. Then they were placed in the most secure part of the prison with their feet fastened in stocks.

Having received this order, he put them into the inner prison and fastened their feet in the stocks (Acts 16:24)

The inner prison was a dungeon with little air and light. Most of the prisoners in the inner prison were awaiting execution, although that was certainly not the case with Paul and Silas. Stocks were wooden frames that securely held the feet so that the prisoner could not move his legs. Such stocks, which were positioned far apart from each other, would cause excruciating discomfort. They were tight and painful. The stocks were intended not only as a security measure, but also as a form of torture.

The missionaries had done nothing wrong. They were not criminals. Yet they still suffered as criminals. After such treatment, one could easily assume that their spirits would be overwhelmed with bitterness and despair. Yet that was not the case at all. They were praying and singing!

About midnight Paul and Silas were praying and singing hymns to God, and the prisoners were listening to them (Acts 16:25)

Wow! Instead of singing the blues, Paul and Silas were singing praises. Like the apostles who were unjustly beaten in Acts 5:41, they rejoiced that they were counted worthy to suffer for Christ.

The attitude of the apostles and early Christians when faced with adversity is truly remarkable. Even when their bodies were bound, their spirits were always free. They found reason to rejoice. Such rejoicing is in accordance with the Lord's words in the Sermon on the Mount: "Blessed are you when others revile you and persecute you and utter all kinds of evil against you falsely on my account. *Rejoice and be glad,* for your reward is great in heaven, for so they persecuted the prophets who were before you" (Matthew 5:11-12, emphasis mine), and Peter's exhortation: "Yet if anyone suffers as a Christian, let him not be ashamed, but let him glorify God in that name" (1 Peter 4:16). The joy of a Christian is not dependent upon circumstances, but exists in spite of them.

Paul's letter to the Philippians is often called "The Epistle of Joy." It was written during his first Roman imprisonment. He was in chains, uncertain of his future, and knew that some preachers were trying to harm him. Yet he found reason to write about joy!

While they were singing, a great earthquake suddenly occurred opening the doors of the prison.

And suddenly there was a great earthquake, so that the foundations of the prison were shaken. And immediately all the doors were opened, and everyone's bonds were unfastened (Acts 16:26)

Although earthquakes were common in the area, there is no doubt this was the work of God. The fact that the earthquake was severe enough to unloose every prisoner without anyone getting hurt proves that to be true. This is not the first time in the book of Acts that disciples were miraculously delivered from their confinement (5:19-26; 12:5-19). The miracle in our present text, however, served to deliver the jailer, not the jailed.

The jailer was awakened by the jolt of the earthquake and the slamming of the prison doors against the stone floors. He ran to the prisoners, saw the doors unlocked, assumed that everyone escaped, and was about to commit suicide.

When the jailor woke and saw that the prison doors were open, he drew his sword and was about to kill himself, supposing that the prisoners had escaped (Acts 16:27)

At that time, jailers were held personally responsible for their prisoners. If a prisoner escaped, the jailer was often put to death as punishment (12:18-19; 27:42). It is no wonder then that the jailer felt so hopeless. He was a dead man!

In Greek and Roman civilizations, it was completely acceptable, and even honorable, to commit suicide when faced with situations that would surely result in death. They thought it was better to take your own life than to let another take it. It is important to note that suicide (self-murder) is condemned in the Bible (Romans 13:9).

As the jailer drew his sword to commit suicide, Paul cried out to stop him. The situation was not as hopeless as it seemed. No one had escaped.

But Paul cried with a loud voice, "Do not harm yourself, for we are all here." And the jailer called for lights and rushed in, and

trembling with fear he fell down before Paul and Silas (Acts 16:28-29)

What a relief! The jailer was spared by a voice in the dark. Everyone was accounted for. The jailer immediately called for lights, secured the prisoners (as the Western Text states), and fell before Paul and Silas. His rough hands were now replaced with trembling feet!

Convinced that the two prisoners before him were men of God, the jailer humbly asked them the question of questions.

Then he brought them out and said, "Sirs, what must I do to be saved?" And they said, "Believe in the Lord Jesus, and you will be saved, you and your household" (Acts 16:30-31)

When the jailer asked how to be saved, Paul and Silas told him to believe in the Lord Jesus. Then they told him the message about Jesus so that he might be saved. Belief in Jesus as the Son of God is absolutely essential to salvation.

And they spoke the word of the Lord to him and to all who were in his house (Acts 16:32)

Some have argued that the jailer was saved at verse 31. That could not be the case, however, because he had never even heard the message about Jesus. Since faith comes by hearing the gospel message (Romans 10:17), he could not have been saved yet.

The two missionaries told the jailer and his household about Jesus. The Lord's birth, teachings, miracles, sacrificial death, and glorious resurrection were no doubt rehearsed that night. Also rehearsed was the plan of salvation, which includes being buried in the waters of baptism for the forgiveness of sins (Acts 2:38; 22:16). This news prompted the jailer to be baptized immediately.

And he took them the same hour of the night and washed their wounds; and he was baptized at once, he and all his family (Acts 16:33)

The jailer washed and was washed! He washed Paul and Silas' wounds from the earlier beating and was himself washed from his sins by the blood of Christ. The fact that baptism took place in the middle of the night indicates that it is very important, and should be done with a sense of urgency. One should not delay or postpone baptism (2:41; 8:12-13, 36; 9:18; 10:48; 16:15).

The late Tolbert Fanning made an excellent observation about the plan of salvation. He wrote, "To the uninstructed Philippian jailor, Paul said, 'Believe, and thou shalt be saved, and thy house,' but to others who had heard, understood, and received the word in their hearts, as the Pentecostians, said the man with the keys, 'Repent,' and to one who had believed and repented, as Saul of Tarsus, one divinely commissioned said, 'Why tarriest thou? Arise, and be baptized and wash way thy sins calling on the name of the Lord.' Thus we have plainly given the gospel conditions of adoption into the heavenly family in their true order." Amen.

As is the case with all the household conversions in the book of Acts, some argue that the jailer's household included infants. We

COMING TO CHRIST | 83

know that was not so, however, because those baptized "believed" (v. 34). Infants cannot believe!

The jailer could have never imagined that two alleged criminals and an earthquake in the middle of the night could change his life forever, but that is exactly what happened. He abandoned idolatry and became a Christian. Like Lydia and Cornelius, the jailer's thankfulness was exhibited through hospitality.

Then he brought them up into his house and set food before them. And he rejoiced along with his entire household that he had believed in God (Acts 16:34)

The eunuch rejoiced after his baptism (Acts 8:39), not before it. Now we see the same thing with the jailor. He could finally rest comfortably knowing that he was right with God.

Although Paul "suffered" and was "shamefully treated" in Philippi (1 Thessalonians 2:2), having been slandered, stripped, beaten, and imprisoned in stocks, his labor was not in vain. Souls were saved and a church was established. He would later refer to the Philippian brethren as his "joy and crown" (Philippians 4:1). After being released from prison, Paul traveled to the city of Thessalonica.

Review
Paul labored in Philippi
Paul cast out demon and was imprisoned
Paul and Silas sang praises at midnight
Earthquake awoke jailor in a panic
Jailer and his household heard message and were baptized

CHAPTER 8

THE CORINTHIANS

Corinth was the capital of the Roman province of Achaia. It was situated on an isthmus (narrow strip of land joining two large bodies) between the Adriatic Sea and the Aegean Sea. It was the leading center of commerce in the region and had two impressive seaports. Corinth was also known for the Isthmian Games, which were held every other year just north of the city and rivaled the Olympics.

Corinth was home to many pagan temples, including the Temple of Aphrodite, the goddess of love. The temple housed over 1,000 prostitutes, who converged upon the city streets at night.

The moral depravity of Corinth has been well documented. It was a cesspool of wicked behavior. In fact, the name Corinth was synonymous with licentiousness. "To live like a Corinthian," "Corinthian girl," and "Corinthianize" were all common expressions used in reference to immorality. That makes the conversion of the Corinthians all the more impressive.

After arriving in Corinth, which was about 50 miles southwest of Athens, Paul met a Jewish man named Aquila and his wife Priscilla. They were tentmakers who had been banished from Italy because of an anti-Semetic stir during the reign of Claudius (A. D. 41-54). Paul, who was also a tentmaker, stayed with the couple while in the city.

And because he was of the same trade he stayed with them

and worked, for they were tentmakers by trade (Acts 18:3)

Paul often worked to support himself making tents while on his journeys (Acts 20:34; 1 Corinthians 4:12; 1 Thessalonians 2:9; 2 Thessalonians 3:8). He had every right to be supported by the brethren, but sometimes forfeited that right to avoid being falsely accused of selfish motives and to be a model of good work ethic (1 Corinthians 9).

Some dispute has occurred about whether or not Aquila and Priscilla were Christians before Paul met them in Corinth. Although it is immaterial, it seems most likely that they were Christians before meeting Paul. (1) There is no record of the couple obeying the gospel when Paul came to Corinth. (2) Paul does not mention them in his list of converts in Corinth in 1 Corinthians 1. (3) It is hard to imagine unbelieving Jews receiving Paul as hospitably as they did.

Aquila and Priscilla, also known as Prisca, became some of Paul's closest friends. They were loyal and trustworthy, and on at least one occasion "risked their necks" for the apostle (Romans 16:4). Interestingly, Aquila and Priscilla are always mentioned together in scripture. Never is one mentioned without the other (Acts 18:2, 18, 26; Romans 16:3; 1 Corinthians 16:19; 2 Timothy 4:19).

It was Paul's custom to visit the synagogue on the Sabbath (13:5, 14; 14:1; 17:1-2; 10, 17; 18:4, 19; 19:8). This was not to observe the Sabbath or any other part of the Old Law, but to convert the Jews to Christ. Corinth was no different.

And he reasoned in the synagogue every Sabbath, and tried to persuade Jews and Greeks (Acts 18:4)

The idea of a crucified Messiah was very different than what most Jews anticipated (1 Corinthians 1:23). They expected the Messiah to be a strong military leader who would return the nation to its prominence. Therefore, it did not take long for tensions to rise between Paul and many in the synagogue. They bitterly opposed the truth proclaimed by the apostle. Knowing that Jesus said, "Do not throw your pearls before pigs" (Matthew 7:6), Paul shook out his garments and went elsewhere.

And when they opposed and reviled him, he shook out his garments and said to them, "Your blood be on your own heads! I am innocent. From now on I will go to the Gentiles" (Acts 18:6)

Jews often shook out their garments as a sign of rejection. This was not the first time Paul had made such a gesture when opposed by unbelieving Jews. When Barnabas and he were expelled from Antioch, they "shook off the dust from their feet against them" (Acts 13:51). This was in accordance with what the Lord told the disciples during his earthly ministry (Luke 9:5; 10:11). It would infuriate the Jews to have that gesture made against them! Paul went next door to a private residence and continued his preaching.

And he left there and went to the house of a man named Titius Justus, a worshiper of God. His house was next to the synagogue (Acts 18:7)

Like Cornelius, Titius Justus was a Gentile worshipper of the true God and was no doubt present in the synagogue when Paul spoke there. He was moved by the words of the apostle and graciously opened his home to him. Once again, we see God working providentially to provide a platform for the message to sound forth. The close proximity of Justus' house to the synagogue would only fan the flames of anger on the part of the Jews.

Among those converted to Christ in Corinth was a man named Crispus. He was a prominent figure in the Jewish community.

Crispus, the ruler of the synagogue, believed in the Lord, together with his entire household (Acts 18:8a)

The ruler of the synagogue was in charge of supervising the services to make sure Jewish tradition was upheld. He was viewed as exceeding others in knowledge and zeal. Therefore, it must have sent a strong message when the ruler gave up his seat to follow Jesus. Crispus was one of the few people Paul personally baptized in Corinth (1 Corinthians 1:14).

One can only imagine how the Jews must have become more and more furious with Paul as his labors continued in Corinth. (1) Paul entered the synagogue and preached that Jesus of Nazareth was the Son of God. (2) He used the Jewish gesture of rejection against the Jews. (3) He declared that he was going to the Gentiles. (4) He began teaching the gospel message at a house that was next door to the synagogue. (5) He converted the ruler of the synagogue.

There is an important lesson to learn here about prejudging who may or may not respond to the gospel message. Who would have thought that a ruler of the synagogue would be converted to Christ? Yet he was. Sometimes those who seem the least likely to obey are the first to do it. If the Sosthenes in 1 Corinthians 1:1 is the same as the Sosthenes in Acts 18:17, Paul may have converted *two* rulers of the synagogue in Corinth!

In addition to Crispus and his household, others rendered their obedience to the gospel. They were baptized into Christ!

And many of the Corinthians hearing Paul believed and were baptized (Acts 18:8b)

Jesus said that those who believe and are baptized will be saved (Mark 16:16). Here we see more people doing just that. The Corinthians became Christians! Notice also that hearing came before belief (Romans 10:17).

Paul would later write at least two letters to the church at Corinth (and probably more — 1 Corinthians 5:9). Since it was through his efforts that the church there was established, he called himself their "father in Christ Jesus" (1 Corinthians 4:15). In addition to Paul, Apollos and Timothy also labored with the church at Corinth.

The phrase "church...in Corinth" is a tremendous paradox, which shows the power of Christ and the gospel. Although the city was given over to wickedness ("sin city"), there was still a light shining through the smog of sin!

Review

Paul entered Corinth

Paul stayed with Aquila and Priscilla

Paul expelled from synagogue

Paul preached next door to synagogue

Crispus and many Corinthians believed and were baptized

CHAPTER 9

THE EPHESIANS

Ephesus was a prominent city in the Roman Empire, behind only Rome, Alexandria, and Antioch of Syria. Its population was estimated to be 250,000 or more. The city was located near the mouth of the Cayster River and had a harbor that could accommodate the largest ships, although river silt was a constant problem.

Ephesus was home to one of the seven wonders of the ancient world — the temple of the goddess Artemis, also called Diana. It also had a theater which seated 24,000 people.

While on his third missionary journey, Paul came to the city of Ephesus and met about twelve men called "disciples."

And it happened that while Apollos was at Corinth, Paul passed through the inland country and came to Ephesus. There he found some disciples (Acts 19:1)

As Paul talked with these men, he asked if they had received the Holy Spirit when they believed. Although "receiving the Holy Spirit" can have different meanings depending upon the context, here it refers to the impartation of the miraculous gifts by the Spirit through the laying on of an apostle's hands (v. 6). They had not.

He said to them, "Did you receive the Holy Spirit when you believed?" And they said, "No, we have not even heard that there

is a Holy Spirit." And he said, "Into what then were you baptized?" They said, "Into John's baptism." And Paul said, "John baptized with the baptism of repentance, telling the people to believe in the one who was to come after him, that is, Jesus" (Acts 19:2-4)

Since the Holy Spirit was spoken of in the Old Testament and by John the baptizer, they surely knew that the Holy Spirit existed. The idea is that they had not heard the Holy Spirit was for them to receive in miraculous measures.

There has been much dispute about what is meant by the term "disciples" in this text. Were they Christians or not? Since they were ignorant of the Holy Spirit and had never been baptized into Christ, we can safely conclude that they were not Christians. These men had received the baptism of John and nothing more.

Paul reminded the men that John, as the prophesied preparer, spoke about one to come after him, namely Jesus. They were then baptized into Jesus immediately.

On hearing this, they were baptized in the name of the Lord Jesus (Acts 19:5)

As noted, these men were not Christians before they were baptized into Jesus. Baptism is not for Christians. It is for those wishing to become Christians. Never do we read about a Christian being baptized in the New Testament.

After their baptism, Paul imparted the miraculous gifts to them. This was done through the laying on of his hands.

And when Paul had laid his hands on them, the Holy Spirit came on them, and they began speaking in tongues and prophesying (Acts 19:6)

Like the Samaritans (Acts 8:17), the Ephesians received a miraculous measure of the Holy Spirit, which allowed them to speak in tongues and prophesy. As noted in chapter 1, tongue speaking allowed the speaker to communicate in languages he had never studied before. The gift of prophesy allowed one to utter divinely revealed truths.

Paul remained in Ephesus for about 3 years proclaiming the message in the synagogue, the hall of Tyrannus, and elsewhere. The church was strong at first, but later left its first love (Revelation 2:4).

Review
Paul entered Ephesus
Paul met twelve disciples
Paul discovered men were disciples of John
Paul proclaimed message to men
Men were baptized and received miraculous gifts

Scriptural Components of Baptism

- Proper Mode — Immersion
- Proper Authority — Name of Christ
- Proper Purpose — Forgiveness of Sins
- Proper Subject — Penitent Believer

CHAPTER 10

ANSWERING ARGUMENTS ABOUT BAPTISM

There are several arguments that people use to deny the necessity of water baptism. We will attempt to answer those arguments now. They are in no particular order.

(1) *We are saved by grace.* All agree that we are saved by grace (Titus 2:11). There is nothing that we can do to earn or merit our salvation. It is a gift from God (Ephesians 2:8). However, grace is appropriated on a conditional basis. If that were not the case then everybody would be saved, which we know is not true (Matthew 7:13-14). Grace is conditioned upon an obedient faith. For instance, Noah was saved from the flood by grace *when* he built an ark of gopher wood (Hebrews 11:7) and the children of Israel were saved from snakebite by grace *when* they looked on the bronze serpent (Numbers 21:9). In both instances, we see that grace was conditioned upon an obedient faith. The same is true with our salvation from sin. For instance, the Jews were saved from sin *when* they repented and were baptized (Acts 2:38).

(2) *Paul was not sent to baptize.* In writing to the brethren at Corinth, Paul stated that he was not sent to baptize, but to preach the gospel (1 Corinthians 1:17). There are several things that must be understood as we seek to determine what is meant by that statement. (1) Jesus commanded the apostles to baptize in the Great Commission (Matthew 28:19). (2) Paul had baptized Crispus, Gaius, and the household of Stephanas at Corinth (1 Corinthians 1:14, 16). (3) Paul wrote many of the passages that emphasize the necessity of baptism (Romans 6:3-5; 1 Corinthians 12:13; Galatians 3:26-27; Colossians 2:12-13). What then did Paul mean when he stated he was not sent to baptize? The context indicates that there was division in the church at Corinth. The brethren were forming sects based on who had baptized them. This must be remembered when interpreting Paul's statement. He was simply saying that the one who does the baptizing is not important.

(3) *The thief on the cross was not baptized.* One can only assume that the thief on the cross was not baptized. He may have been baptized by John (Matthew 3:5-6) or by the disciples of the Lord (John 4:1). We do not know. However, it does not matter whether the thief was baptized or not because he lived under the Old Law, before Christ shed his blood and before the baptism of Christ was commanded. Furthermore, the thief, being a Jew, was already in the covenant relationship. So he was an erring child of God, not an alien sinner. Therefore, the thief on the cross is an invalid argument.

(4) *We are saved by the blood.* All agree that we are saved by the precious blood of Christ (Ephesians 1:7; 1 Peter 1:18-19). Without the shedding of his blood, we would have no hope of redemption. However, there must be a point when the blood of Christ is applied or contacted. When is that? The blood is applied when we are baptized. For instance, the scriptures teach that the blood remits sin (Matthew 26:28), washes away sin (Revelation 1:5), cleanses us (1 John 1:7), and saves us (Romans 5:9). The scriptures also teach that baptism remits sin (Acts 2:38), washes away sin (Acts 22:16), cleanses us (Ephesians 5:26), and saves us (1 Peter 3:21). How can those passages be reconciled? The only logical explanation is that we contact the blood when we are baptized. In other words, the blood is *what* saves us; baptism is *when* it saves us. Only those baptized in water are saved by the blood!

(5) *Mark 16:16 refers to Holy Spirit baptism.* Bible students recognize that Mark 16:16 and Matthew 28:19 are parallel accounts. Both are records of the same event — the Great Commission. By looking at Matthew's account, we see that the baptism under consideration is administered by man and is "in the name of." Is Holy Spirit baptism administered by man and "in the name of?" No. Is water baptism administered by man and "in the name of?" Yes. Therefore, we must conclude that the baptism of Mark 16:16 is water baptism. Only water baptism was commanded for all people (Acts 10:47-48).

(6) *Mark 16:16 does not say "and is baptized not."* Suppose someone said, "He that eats and digests shall live, but he that eats not shall die." Would it be necessary to add the phrase "and digests not?" No. If one does not eat he will not digest. The same is true with Mark 16:16. If one does not believe he will not be baptized. Therefore, it was not necessary for the Lord to add the phrase "and is baptized not." Furthermore, if the Lord had added the phrase "and is baptized not," he would have made belief and baptism necessary for salvation and non-belief and non-baptism necessary for damnation, leaving two groups of people neither saved nor damned. Think about it. What about those who believed but were not baptized? What about those who were baptized but did not believe? They would not fall into either category. Mark 16:16 is worded just right. One must believe and be baptized to be saved, while all unbelievers will be damned.

(7) *Mark 16:16 is not authentic.* Some argue that Mark's original gospel concluded at verse 8, and that the last 12 verses were added later. If that were true, however, Mark's gospel would have ended with the disciples "afraid." Who can believe such a thing? Furthermore, many ancient manuscripts, including Codices Alexandrian and Washington, have the latter verses, and many ancient writers, including Justin Martyr and Irenaeus, quote from the latter verses in their works, which predate the manuscript evidence. Mark 16:16 is authentic!

(8) *We are not saved by works.* There are different kinds of works mentioned in the New Testament. We read about works of the Law of Moses (Galatians 2:16), works of the flesh (Galatians 5:19-21), works of the devil (1 John 3:8), works of darkness (Ephesians 5:11), and works of men (2 Timothy 1:9). All agree that we are not saved by any of those works. However, belief is a work (John 6:28-29). So there is a kind of work involved in our salvation from sin. It is "the work of God," which includes faith, repentance, confession, and baptism.

We have answered eight arguments used to deny the necessity of baptism. None of the arguments are valid. Baptism in water is necessary for salvation from sin (Mark 16:16; John 3:5; Acts 2:38; 22:16; Romans 6:3-5; Galatians 3:26-27; Colossians 2:12-13; 1 Peter 3:21).

Baptism Stands Between

Mark 16:16 — Sinner/Salvation

Acts 2:38 — Sinner/Remission

Acts 22:16 — Sinner/Washed

Romans 6:3 — Sinner/Death of Christ

Galatians 3:27 — Sinner/Putting on Christ

KJV

Ephesians	**Cornelius**
Heard	Heard
(Eph. 1:13)	(Acts 10:33)
↓	↓
Believed	Believed
(Eph. 1:13)	(Acts 15:7)
↓	↓
Repented	Repented
(Acts 20:21)	(Acts 11:18)
↓	↓
Baptized	Baptized
(Acts 19:5)	(Acts 10:48)
↓	↓
Saved by Grace	Saved by Grace
(Eph. 2:8)	(Acts 15:11)

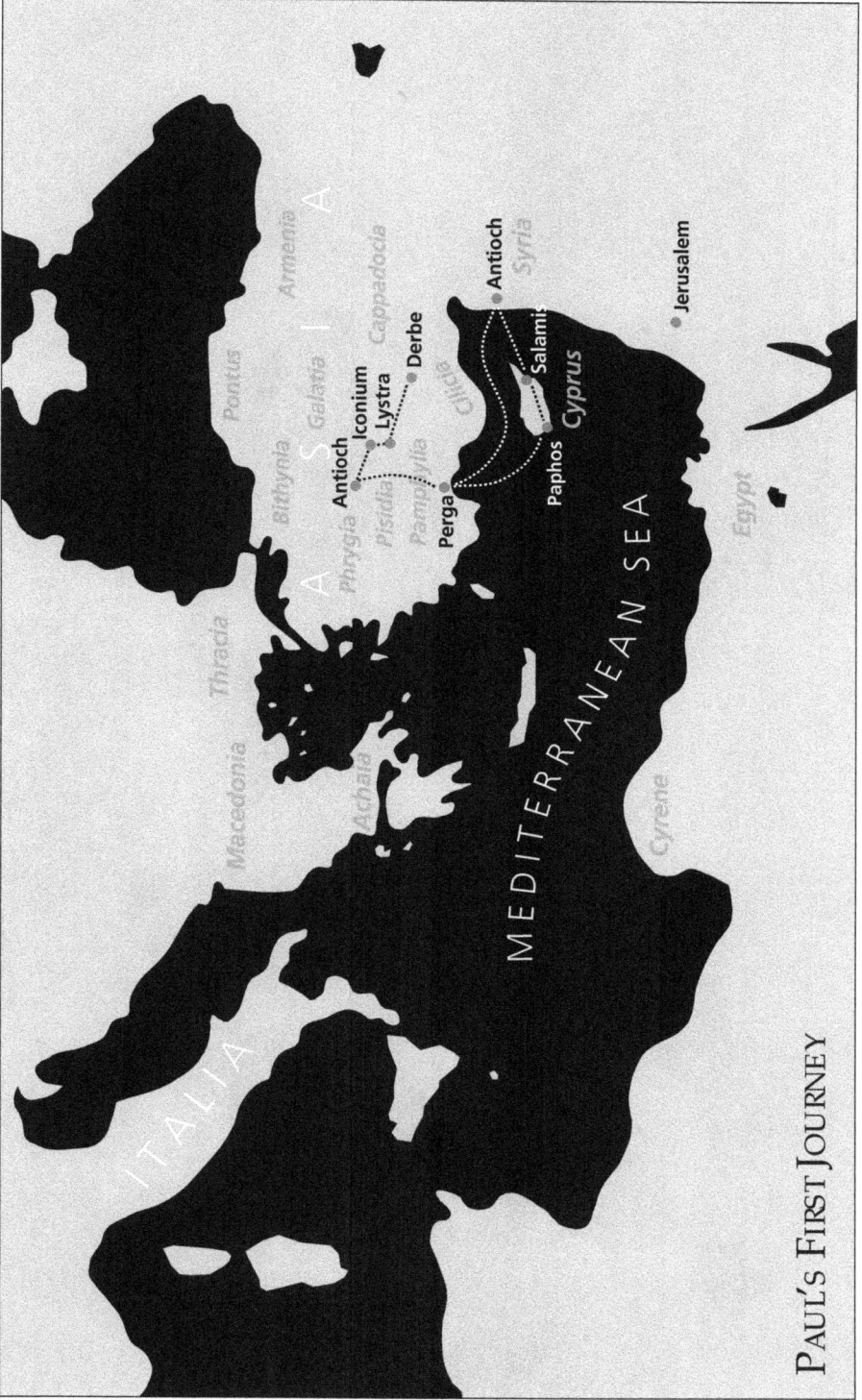

PAUL'S FIRST JOURNEY

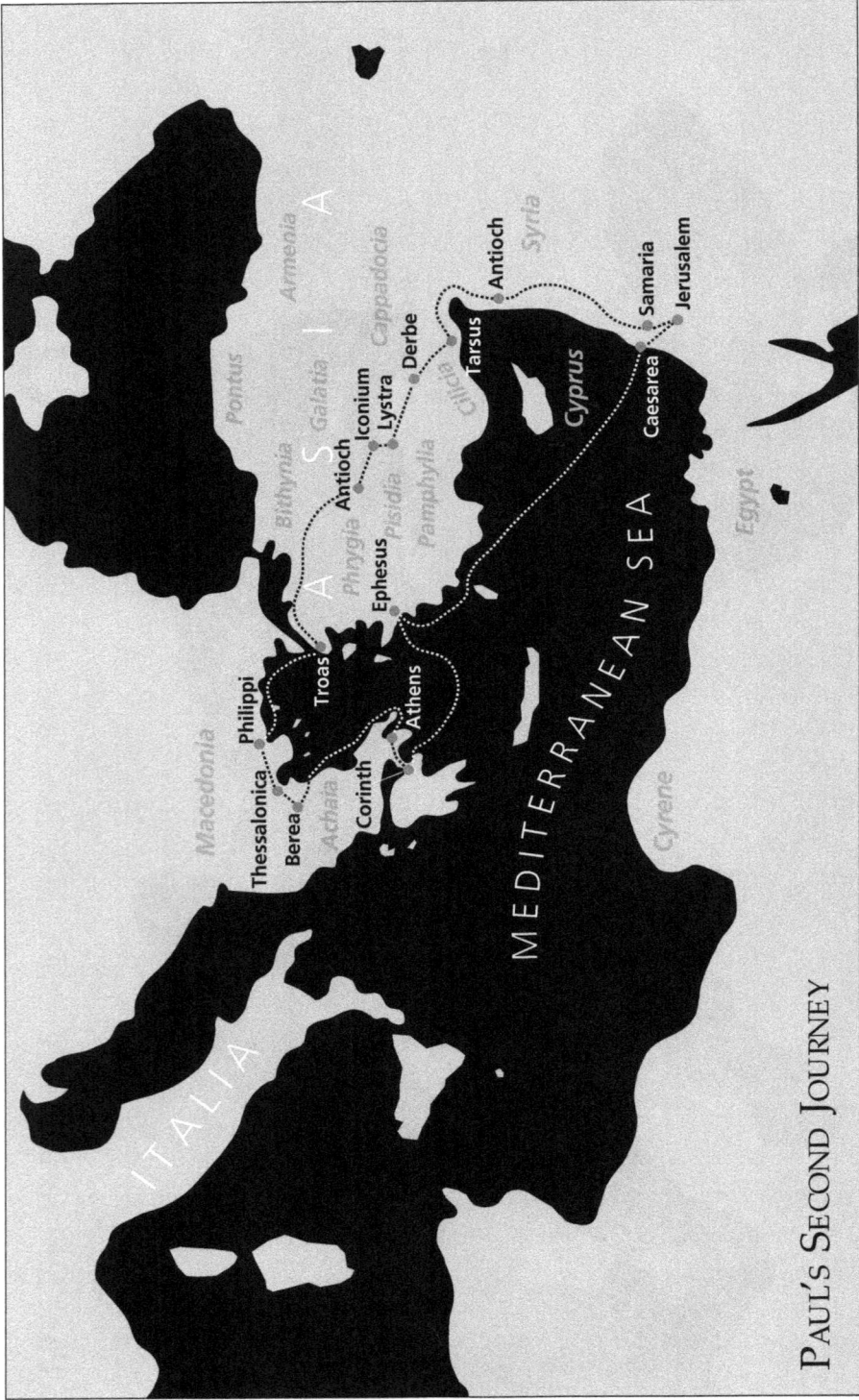

PAUL'S SECOND JOURNEY

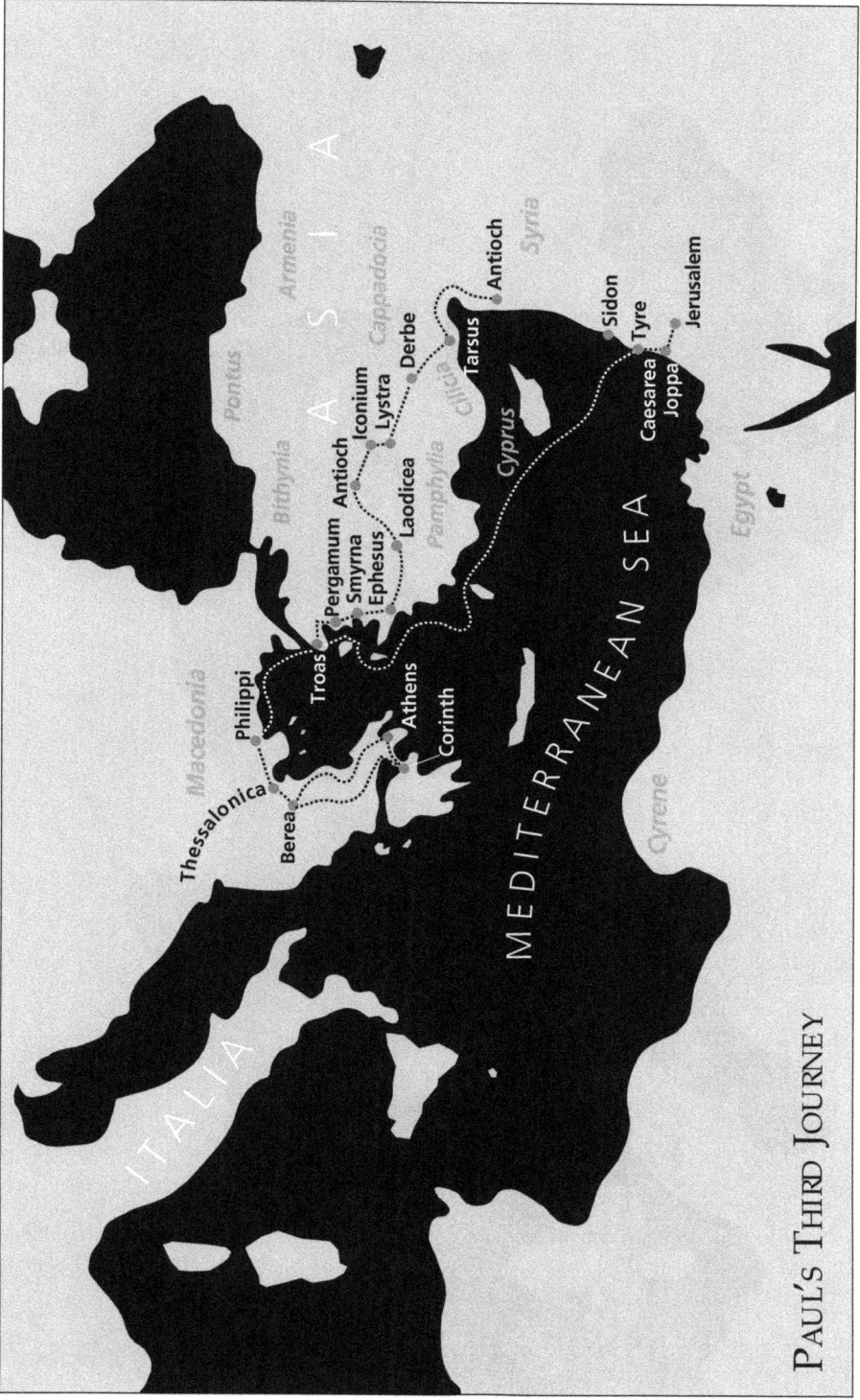

PAUL'S THIRD JOURNEY

PAUL'S FOURTH JOURNEY

Special Thanks

Paula Adams, Kathy Paugh
and Stephen Sebree

EP

ERHARDT PUBLICATIONS

ErhardtPublications.com

NOTES

NOTES

www.ingramcontent.com/pod-product-compliance
Lightning Source LLC
Chambersburg PA
CBHW031341040426

42443CB00006B/423